D0441562

Dependency and Development in Latin America

Dependency and Development in Latin America

Fernando Henrique Cardoso
and Enzo Faletto

Translated by Marjory Mattingly Urquidi

UNIVERSITY OF CALIFORNIA PRESS

BERKELEY · LOS ANGELES · LONDON

This is an expanded and emended version of
Dependencia y desarrollo en América Latina
(Siglo Veintiuno Editores, SA, 1971).

University of California Press
Berkeley and Los Angeles, California
University of California Press, Ltd.
London, England

ISBN 0–520–03193–8 (cloth)
    0–520–03527–5 (paper)
Library of Congress Catalog Card Number: 75–46033
Printed in the United States of America
Designed by Dave Comstock

8 9

Contents

Preface to the English Edition

We wrote this book in Santiago, Chile, between 1965 and the first months of 1967. At that time, we worked at the Latin American Institute for Economic and Social Planning, a United Nations organization which originated from the Economic Commission for Latin America (ECLA). Our purpose was to show specifically *how* social, political, and economic development are related in Latin America.

Several studies on dependency by Latin Americans have affected the academic community and even broader audiences. There are numerous discussions in the United States on the contributions and weaknesses of what has been called "dependency theory." In Europe also, with perhaps less enthusiasm, these studies were subject to debate. African economists, influenced by Marxist analysis, and to some extent by Latin American thought on dependency, have also proposed models for the interpretation of African and Asian development. Reviewing the large bibliography on this subject ten years after the draft version of this essay, it seems timely to clarify how we perceive dependency as a practical and theoretical problem. We give special consideration in this preface to the methodology used in our book.

Outside Latin America, the academic community in the United States elaborated scientific explanatory models of the different socio-cultural dimensions of society. Examples can be found in the structural-functionalist paradigms proposed by Merton or Parsons, in theories of political behavior (as in Easton's systemic analysis and in Laswell's efforts to characterize dimensions of power and influence), and even in several theories of modernization and political development. The influence of these explanatory models started to increase in Latin America in the fifties and achieved "scientific respectability" in the sixties. These paradigms inspired several theories on Latin American development processes.

At the same time, economists at ECLA[1] were proposing a critical view of development. They criticized conservative economists who believed that the present division of labor in the world market was inevitable because it was based on "comparative advantages": some countries would be better endowed to produce raw materials, whereas others would have advantages in producing industrial goods. In spite of their critical nature, ECLA economic theories and critiques were not based on an analysis of social process, did not call attention to imperialist relationships among countries, and did not take into account the asymmetric relations between classes.

Consequently a counter-critique which cited the narrowness of the ECLA approach also spread through Latin America. It arose, at times implicitly, within ECLA itself, in studies dealing with the concentration of benefits from technological

1. Economic Commission for Latin America (ECLA), or CEPAL, as it is known in the Latin American countries, is a United Nations organization. ECLA's economic staff proposed a paradigm for the analysis of development, which became the most influential theory in Latin American social sciences since the early fifties.

progress, as well as in essays on the social conditions of development by Medina Echeverría. It is also implicit in the work of intellectuals in the universities and political movements (in São Paulo, Mexico, Buenos Aires, or Caracas) who emphasized the inequalities of wealth and opportunity inherent in a development that derives from capitalist expansion and the strengthening of imperialism.

Our essay belongs to that more radically critical Latin American heritage. We attempt to reestablish the intellectual tradition based on a comprehensive social science. We seek a global and dynamic understanding of social structures instead of looking only at specific dimensions of the social process. We oppose the academic tradition which conceived of domination and socio-cultural relations as "dimensions," analytically independent of one another, and together independent of the economy, as if each one of these dimensions corresponded to separate spheres of reality. In that sense, we stress the socio-political nature of the economic relations of production, thus following the nineteenth-century tradition of treating economy as political economy. This methodological approach, which found its highest expression in Marx, assumes that the hierarchy that exists in society is the result of established ways of organizing the production of material and spiritual life. This hierarchy also serves to assure the unequal appropriation of nature and of the results of human work by social classes and groups. So we attempt to analyze domination in its connection with economic expansion.

There is a difference of a methodological nature between the approach followed by us in this essay and the others mentioned above. We use a dialectical approach to study society, its structures and processes of change. It will be useful for the reader if we spell out some basic elements of this methodological approach.

Dialectics and the Analysis of Structures and Processes

A basic assumption is that the analysis of social life is fruitful only if it starts from the presupposition that there are relatively stable global structures. However, these structures can be conceived and analyzed in different ways.

For us it is necessary to recognize from the beginning that social structures are the product of man's collective behavior. Therefore, although enduring, social structures can be, and in fact are, continuously transformed by social movements. Consequently, our approach is both structural and historical: it emphasizes not just the structural conditioning of social life, but also the historical transformation of structures by conflict, social movements, and class struggles. Thus our methodology is historical-structural.

This point deserves further attention. The emphasis on the structural aspect can convey the impression that situations of dependency are stable and permanent. This impression, left by faulty analyses, can also suggest that situations of dependency are continuously and necessarily generating more underdevelopment and dependency.

Our approach of course assumes and demonstrates that in the kind of societies for which this mode of analysis is useful, structures are based neither on egalitarian relationships nor on collaborative patterns of social organization. On the contrary, they are founded on social asymmetries and on exploitative types of social organization. Furthermore, it is assumed that an understanding of the strong inequalities characterizing these social structures, as well as an explanation of the exploitative processes through which these structures are maintained, require the analysis of the system of production and the institutions of appropriation, that is, the socio-economic base of society. Finally, in the approach here proposed a central role is assigned to the analysis of the mechanisms and processes of domination through which existing structures are maintained.

But to use this approach to point out only the self-perpetuating structural mechanisms implies neglect of the contradictory results of the very process of development as well as the *possibilities* of negation of the existing order also inherent in social processes. It is therefore useful to remember that forms of dependency can change and to identify the structural possibilities for change, pinpointing the alternatives to dependency existing at any given historical moment.

In other words, our approach should bring to the forefront both aspects of social structures: the mechanisms of self-perpetuation and the possibilities for change. Social structures impose limits on social processes and reiterate established forms of behavior. However, they also generate contradictions and social tensions, opening the possibilities for social movements and ideologies of change. The analyses have to make explicit not only structural constraints that reinforce the reiterative aspects of the reproduction of society, but have also to delineate chances for change, rooted in the very social interest and ideologies created by the development of a given structure. In this process, subordinated social groups and classes, as well as dominated countries, try to counterattack dominant interests that sustain structures of domination.

It is not irrelevant in these attempts to pay attention to ideologies and to intellectual capacity to assess possibilities for change. In decisive historical moments, political capacity (which includes organization, will, and ideologies) is necessary to enforce or to change a structural situation. Intellectual evaluation of a given situation and ideas about what is to be done are crucial in politics. The latter is immersed in the shady area between social interests and human creativity. At that level, gambles more than certainty line the paths through which social forces try to maintain or to change structures. Briefly, in spite of structural "determination," there is room for alternatives in history. Their actualization will depend not just on basic contradictions between interests, but also on the perception of new ways of turning a historical corner through "a passion for the possible."[2]

One final comment about general implications of the methodology used in this book with respect to problems of measurement would be useful. The question is not whether

2. Expression borrowed by Albert Hirschman from Kierkegaard. See Hirschman, Albert, *A Bias for Hope* (New Haven: Yale University Press, 1971), p. 27.

to measure. The question is rather what and how to measure, and also concerns the methodological status of measuring. Characterizing dependency is like characterizing "capitalism," "slavery," or "colonialism." It would make no sense to compare slavery in the southern United States with slavery in the Antilles or in Brazil only in order to assess "degrees of slavery" varying from minus to plus. It would make more sense to compare the slave economy with wage sectors, or slavery in the plantation system with slavery in domestic households, or to investigate the limits imposed by slavery on capitalistic expansion in the United States, Brazil, or the Antilles.

Similarly, there would be little sense in attempting to measure "degrees of dependency," making formal comparisons of dependent situations. Some efforts in that direction have resulted in the isolation of "power dimensions" involved in dependency situations from its "economic aspects." In such a procedure, the very basic characteristic of dependency studies—the emphasis on global analysis—disappears. On the other hand, very often in studies that have been done, each one of the selected dimensions of dependency is conceived in a rather static way to adjust realities to methodological requirements of the "logic of scientific investigation." For instance: when foreign capitals start to promote industrial development in dependent economies some deepening of internal markets occurs and some forms of income redistribution benefits upper levels of middle sectors. In previous forms of dependency—without local industrialization based on multinational enterprises—such a "redistributive process" was not present. In spite of these differences and in spite of the complexity of emergent situations of dependency, some studies in which "dependency theories" were tested assumed that *all* forms of dependency had common features. The rationale behind such a methodology is based on the possible common effect of a general (thus for us "abstract") form of dependency that permeates *all* types of situations. In a dialectical approach such a vague statement is not acceptable. The basic methodological steps in dialectical analyses require an effort to specify each new situation in the search for differences and diversity, and to relate them to the old forms of dependency, stressing, when necessary, even its contradictory aspects and effects.

Thus, before measuring, previous elaboration of adequate theories and categories is required to give sense to data. Certainly, evidence confirming or rejecting particular analysis oriented by a dependency approach has to be taken into account if it has been established on adequate theoretical grounds. But data have to be interpreted in the historical-structural context.

Finally, the methodological status of measurement in a dialectical approach does not play the role of a fundamental device in the logic of demonstration, as if we were dealing with hypotheses to be accepted or rejected only after statistical tests. Of course, in rendering dialectical analysis less abstract (thus less general) and more concrete (thus relating specific sets of relations one to the others) statistical information and demonstrations are useful and necessary. But the crucial questions for demonstration are of a different nature. First of all, it is necessary to propose concepts able to explain trends of change. This implies the recognition of opposing forces which drag history ahead. Second, it is necessary to relate these forces in a global way, characterizing the basic sources of their existence, continuity, and change, by determining forms of domination and forces opposed to them. So, without the concept of capital as the result of exploitation of one class by another it is not possible to explain the movement of capitalist society. Without assuming (and analyzing) forms of dependency, when the studies refer to peripheral countries, it is not possible to render analyses more concrete. It is through the elaboration of key concepts of that type that dialectical analyses explain historical movement in its "totality." That is to say: history becomes understandable when interpretations propose categories strong enough to render clear the fundamental relations that sustain and those that oppose a given structural situation in its globality.

The accuracy of a historical-structural interpretation has to be checked by confronting its delineation of structural conditions and trends of change with actual socio-political process. Both in the construction of interpretation and in its practical validation, realities are at stake: data are not incorporated into the analysis as if they were statically given; the important thing is how they change as social process develops. Significant data are those that illuminate trends of change and emerging processes in history in unanticipated ways. Their "verification" depends on the capacity of social movements to implement what are perceived as structural possibilities. This process depends, on the other hand, on real social and political struggle. So the "demonstration" of an interpretation follows real historical process very closely and depends to some extent on its own ability to show socio-political actors the possible solutions to contradictory situations.

Structural Dependency

For our historical-structural analysis the crucial methodological question was to delineate moments of significant structural change in countries characterized by different situations of dependency in Latin America rather than criticizing on theoretical grounds either the structural approach to socio-economic development proposed by ECLA or the structural functionalist models prevailing in sociological analyses, or blaming vulgar Marxism or the theory of political modernization.

In mechanistic conceptions of history, Latin American economies are perceived as having always been determined by the "capitalist system," as it has developed on a global scale. Fundamental periods of change at the international level, it is contended, marked the significant moments of transformation of Latin American economies. In these interpretations, general characteristics of capitalism replace concrete analyses of specific characteristics of dependent societies. "Mercantilism," "free enterprise and free competition," "monopoly capitalism" are, in general, molds from which historical landmarks of peripheral countries are drawn. Obviously, Latin American societies have been built as a consequence of the expansion of European and American capitalism. Although less obvious, there also are features of capitalism common to developed and dependent countries. However, by excluding from the explanatory model social struggles and the particular relations (economic, social, and political) that give momentum to specific dominated societies, these kinds of interpretation oversimplify history and lead to error: they do not offer accurate characterizations of social structures, nor do they grasp the dynamic aspect of history actualized by social struggles in dependent societies.

If the interpretation only recognizes that mercantilism was an important element in the expansion of commercial capitalism and deduces from this that Latin America was *capitalist,* the content of what happened historically disappears into the vagueness of this abstract statement. The important task is to explain *how* the mercantilist economic drive led to the creation in several parts of Latin America of slave "capitalist" economies, in other parts to the exploitation of indigenous populations, and in some regions, as in southern parts of the continent, to an economy based on wage earners. In every one of those situations, capitalism, in its mercantilist form, was behind the local economies. They were never "feudal" societies. But this is not sufficient to explain the concrete differences between, let us say, Brazilian slave plantations and the Argentinian economy in the nineteenth century. Both were "capitalistic" economies, but they were organized around different relations of production: slavery in one case and relations that developed into almost capitalistic forms of production in the other.

In this book, we do not pretend to derive mechanically significant phases of dependent societies only from the "logic of capitalistic accumulation." We do not see dependency and imperialism as external and internal sides of a single coin, with the internal aspects reduced to the condition of "epiphenomenal." Conceived in this manner, imperialism turns into an active and metaphysical principle which traces out the paths of history on the sensitive but passive skin of dependent countries. Forms of local societies, reactions against imperialism, the political dynamic of local societies, and attempts at alternatives are not taken into consideration. This type of analysis, although it uses Marxist vocabulary, is methodologically symmetrical to interpretations based on the "logic of industrialism," or on the "stages of modernization," or even on the phases of "political development," which foresee change as a result of mechanical factors.

We conceive the relationship between external and internal forces as forming a complex whole whose structural links are not based on mere external forms of exploitation and coercion, but are rooted in coincidences of interests between local dominant classes and international ones, and, on the other side, are challenged by local dominated groups and classes. In some circumstances, the networks of coincident or reconciled interests might expand to include segments of the middle class, if not even of alienated parts of working classes. In other circumstances, segments of dominant classes might seek internal alliance with middle classes, working classes, and even peasants, aiming to protect themselves from foreign penetration that contradicts their interests. External domination in situations of national dependency (opposed to purely colonial situations where the oppression by external agents is more direct) implies the possibility of the "internalization of external interests."

Of course, imperialist penetration is a result of external social forces (multinational enterprises, foreign technology, international financial systems, embassies, foreign states and armies, etc.). What we affirm simply means that the system of domination reappears as an "internal" force, through the social practices of local groups and classes which try to enforce foreign interests, not precisely because they are foreign, but because they may coincide with values and interests that these groups pretend are their own.

Our analyses of concrete situations require us to find out what forms of social and economic exploitation there are, to what degree industrialization and capital accumulation in the periphery has advanced, how local economies relate to the international market, and so forth; and this as the result not only of an abstract "logic of capital accumulation" but also of particular relationships and struggles between social classes and groups at the international as well as at the local level. It is true that local socio-political process, as well as local economic organization, insofar as we are dealing with dependent societies, supposes and reproduces the general features of capitalism as it exists on a global scale. Hence, capital concentration by multinational companies and the monopoly of technological progress in the hands of enterprises located in the center of the international system are obligatory points of reference for the analysis.

The very existence of an economic "periphery" cannot be understood without reference to the economic drive of advanced capitalist economies, which were responsible for the formation of a capitalist periphery and for the integration of traditional noncapitalist economies into the world market. Yet, the expansion of capitalism in Bolivia and Venezuela, in Mexico or Peru, in Brazil and Argentina, in spite of having been submitted to the same global dynamic of international capitalism, did not have the same history or consequences. The differences are rooted not only in the diversity of natural resources, nor just in the different periods in which these economies have been incorporated into the international system (although these factors have played some role). Their explanation must also lie in the different moments at which sectors of local classes allied or clashed with foreign interests, organized different forms of state, sustained distinct ideologies, or tried to implement various policies or defined alternative strategies to cope with imperialist challenges in diverse moments of history.

Interpretations in this book attempt to characterize, in a general manner, the history of that diversity. Of course, there are common factors in capitalism which affect all economies under consideration and which constitute the starting point of the analysis. But it is the diversity within unity that explains historical process. If the analytical effort succeeds, general platitudes and reaffirmations about the role of capitalist modes of production can turn into a lively knowledge of real processes. It is necessary to elaborate concepts and explanations able to show how general trends of capitalist expansion turn into concrete relations among men, classes, and states in the periphery. This is the methodological movement constituting what is called the passage from an "abstract" style of analysis into a "concrete" form of historical knowledge. In that sense, the history of capital accumulation is the history of class struggles, of political movements, of the affirmation of ideologies, and of the establishment of forms of domination and reactions against them.

So, the analysis of structural dependency aims to explain the interrelationships of classes and nation-states at the level of the international scene as well as at the level internal to each country. Dialectical analysis of that complex process includes formulation of concepts linked to the effort to explain how internal and external processes of political domination relate one to the other. It cannot be conceived as if considerations of external factors or foreign domination were enough to explain the dynamic of societies. The real question lies in the interrelationships at both levels. Emphasis has to be laid not only on compatibilities but also on contradictions between these two levels.

Basic Situations of Dependency

We describe two dependency situations that prevailed prior to the present system of international capitalism based on the dynamism of multinational corporations: dependency where the productive system was nationally controlled, and dependency in enclave situations. The important question in comparing these situations is not just whether power is exercized by local entrepreneurs or by "enclave" types of foreign companies, nor just what forms of accumulation and circuits of capital realization there are. The real question is what the *relationship* between these two dimensions is, and what their interaction is with capital accumulation on a global scale.

In enclave economies, foreign invested capital *originates in the exterior,* is incorporated into local productive processes, and transforms parts of itself into wages and taxes. Its value is increased by the exploitation of local labor forces, which transform nature and produce goods that *realize* again the life of this capital when staples (oil, copper, bananas, etc.) are sold in the *external market.*[3]

In economies controlled by local bourgeoisie, the circuit of capital is formally just the opposite. Accumulation is the result of the appropriation of natural resources by local entrepreneurs and the exploitation of the labor force by this same local group. The starting point for capital accumulation is thus *internal.* The process of capital valorization also takes place in the local productive process, but insofar as merchandise consists of staples and food products, the *international market* is required to realize the final steps of the capital circuit.

The case of contemporary dependent industrializing economies[4] controlled by multinational corporations gives the impression of a return to the enclave type of economy. However, although initial accumulation often results from external investment (though not necessarily, because multinational corporations do often use local funds to invest), there is an important difference vis-à-vis enclave economies: a substantial part of industrial production is sold in the *internal market.* A foreign-owned car plant settled in Mexico City or in São Paulo, Brazil, sells most of its production in local

3. In the case of enclave economies, one must distinguish between situations in which foreign enterprises assume control of enterprises that have been created and expanded by local entrepreneurs (e.g., copper mining in Chile) and situations that were originated by foreign investment. These two forms provoke distinct consequences with respect to the formation, role, and political influence of social classes.

4. This last process, being recent, could not be analyzed by classical studies on capitalism. It was foreseen in the case of Czarist Russia by some authors. But Russian development evolved in an entirely different international economic context.

markets. Up to now, exports toward center economies have played a minimal role in the economic strategies of multinational industrial corporations settled in the periphery— rarely surpassing 3 percent of total production.

So, the *forms* adopted by dependency may vary considerably. This variation in form is expressed in the sociopolitical context through the size and type of the working class as well as of the bourgeoisie, the size and type of "middle class," the weight of bureaucracies, the role of the armies, forms of state, the ideologies underlying social movements, and so forth. This book tries to analyze these movements, and dialectical methods, as we have said, demand an attempt at concreteness with regard to the abstract forms of "capital expansion." So we must analyze the diversity of classes, fractions of classes, groups, organizations, and political and ideological movements which form, in a lively and dynamic way, the history of capitalistic expansion in Latin America. In fact, it is through socio-political structures sustained and moved by social classes and groups with opposed interests that capital, as an economic "form" (with its "logic of expansion") is realized in history. Historical-structural analysis illuminates the basic trends through which capital expansion occurs and finds its limits as a socio-political process. In that sense, the understanding of capitalist development requires the analyses of social classes and political context that allow or prevent the actualization of different forms and phases of capital accumulation.

Theory of Dependency and Capitalistic Development

From the economic point of view a system is dependent when the accumulation and expansion of capital cannot find its essential dynamic component inside the system. In capitalistic economies the crucial component for the drive to expand is the capacity to enlarge the scale of capital. This cannot be done without the creation of new technologies and continuous expansion of the production of "capital goods," that is, machinery and equipment, to permit the continuing growth of enterprise expansion and capital accumulation. Furthermore, the expansion of a capitalistic economy requires financial support through a solid banking system. Of course, not all capitalist economies have these capabilities. Some of them have to find on a world scale the necessary complementarity to continue their march toward economic growth.

Almost all contemporary national economic systems are articulated in the international system. Superficial or apologetic analysts, in order to minimize exploitative aspects of the international economy, have merely assumed that "modern" economies are "interdependent." By stating this platitude, they often forget that the important question is what forms that "interdependency" takes. While some national economies need raw material produced by unskilled labor, or industrial goods produced by cheap labor, others need to import equipment and capital goods in general. While some economies become indebted to the financial capital cities of the world, others are creditors. Of course, bankers need clients, as much as clients need bankers. But the "interrelationship" between the two is qualitatively distinct because of the position held by each partner in the structure of the relationship. The same is true for the analysis of "interdependent" economies in world markets.

Capitalism is a world system. But some of its parts have more than their share of leadership and an almost exclusive possession of sectors crucial to production and capital accumulation, such as the technological or financial sectors. They require complementarity from dependent economies, but the crucial elements for the capital expansion on a cumulative and amplified scale are at their disposal.

Peripheral economies, even when they are no longer restricted to the production of raw material, remain dependent in a very specific form: their capital-goods production sectors are not strong enough to ensure continuous advance of the system, in financial as well as in technological and organizational terms. So, in order to go ahead with economic expansion, a dependent country has to play the "interdependency" game, but in a position similar to the client who approaches a banker. Of course, clients usually develop strategies of independence and can try to use the borrowed money in productive ways. But insofar as there are structural border lines, successful attempts are not an automatic output of the game. More often, rules of domination are enforced, and even if the dependent country becomes less poor after the first loan, a second one follows. In most cases, when such an economy flourishes, its roots have been planted by those who hold the lending notes.

Characterization of contemporary forms of dependent development could be perhaps the most significant contribution by "dependentistas" to the theory of capitalistic societies. If there is any novelty in this essay, it consists, together with the characterization of past forms of dependency, in the attempt to delineate what has been called "the new dependency." By means of this analysis it was foreseen how a general trend (industrial capitalism) creates concrete situations of dependency with features distinct from those of advanced capitalist societies. So, peripheral industrialization is based on products which in the center are *mass consumed,* but which are typically *luxurious consumption* in dependent societies. Industrialization in dependent economies enhances income concentration as it increases sharp differences in productivity without generalizing this trend to the whole of the economy: whereas the production of cars, televisions, refrigerators, and like types of goods is based on modern technology, important parts of food products, textiles, and other goods that constitute the basic consumption for the masses are still based on more traditional technology and relations of production. The wages of technicians, managers, and specialized workers, although not directly determined by productivity, are incomparably higher than those earned by peasants or workers employed in traditional sectors. Thus, industrialization in the periphery increases disparity of income among wage earners accentuating what has been called in Latin America the "structural heterogeneity."

These considerations stress that dependent capitalistic economies are not identical to central capitalistic economies. In spite of that, we do not subscribe to the attempts that have been made to propose a "theory of dependent capitalism." Of course, analyses of situations of dependency imply theories and require the use of methodologies. But—even by definition—it seems senseless to search for "laws of movement" specific to situations that *are dependent*, that is, that have their main features determined by the phases and trend of expansion of capitalism on a world scale. Attempts have to be made to enlarge and to give more specificity to the laws that have been developed and are being brought up to date by authors interested in the analysis of a general economic theory of capitalism. Our contribution, if there is one, goes in that direction without any pretentious aim to propose new theories that depart from the classical ones. To avoid misinterpretations, we refer to "situations of dependency" rather than to the "category" or to the "theory" of dependency.

A real process of dependent development does exist in some Latin American countries. By development, in this context, we mean "capitalist development." This form of development, in the periphery as well as in the center, produces as it evolves, in a cyclical way, wealth and poverty, accumulation and shortage of capital, employment for some and unemployment for others. So, we do not mean by the notion of "development" the achievement of a more egalitarian or more just society. These are not consequences expected from capitalist development, especially in peripheral economies.

By pointing to the existence of a process of capitalistic expansion in the periphery, we make a double criticism. We criticize those who expect permanent stagnation in underdeveloped dependent countries because of a constant decline in the rate of profit or the "narrowness of internal markets," which supposedly function as an insurpassable obstacle to capitalistic advancement. But we also criticize those who expect capitalistic development of peripheral economies to solve problems such as distribution of property, full employment, better income distribution, and better living conditions for people. Even in developed economies these problems remain unsolved, as Puerto Ricans, blacks, and poor whites testify in America. It would be unrealistic (if not apologetic) to believe that the existence of an actual process of capitalistic development in the peripheral economies will suppress social problems and conflicts around them. Development, in this context, means the progress of productive forces, mainly through the import of technology, capital accumulation, penetration of local economies by foreign enterprises, increasing numbers of wage-earning groups, and intensification of social division labor. It is realistic to expect either a shifting of the arena in which struggles are present or the unfolding of issues around which conflicts will be at stake. It is not realistic to imagine that capitalist development will solve basic problems for the majority of the population. In the end, what has to be discussed as an alternative is not the consolidation of the state and the fulfillment of "autonomous capitalism," but how to supercede them. The important question, then, is how to construct paths toward socialism.

We have limited our analyses to forms of dependency within capitalistic societies and, furthermore, to situations in which a nation-state has been formed. Although there are forms of dependent relationships between socialist countries, the structural context that permits an understanding of these is quite different from that within capitalist countries and requires specific analyses. The same is also true for economies like the Indian economy—and, to a lesser extent, that of Japan—which have historical patterns of formation that cannot be explained by the unfolding of European or American capitalistic economic expansion, although they also became linked, later on, to the international market.

We have not intended to discuss colonial types of contemporary situations of dependency in Latin America, such as, in the purest example, Puerto Rico. Considerable intellectual work has to be done to specify and render understand-able, in the context of a more general view about dependency, the particularities of colonial or almost colonial situations. This book has not the pretension to exhaust or even to deal with all the forms of dependency that occur even in Latin America.

F. H. C. and E. F.
1976

CHAPTER ONE
Introduction

A̲t the end of World War II, some Latin American countries seemed about to form their industrial sector and to begin economic changes that would lead to self-sustained growth.

Production and markets had been reorganized in the wake of the 1929 depression, and some Latin American economies had accumulated large amounts of foreign exchange and had benefited from the wartime protection of domestic markets selling staples and even industrialized products abroad, with no corresponding possibility of importing merchandise, because American and European economies were devoted to the war effort. They seemed to be on the verge of closing the cycle known as "import substitution,"[1]

1. Concerning the need for industrialization to supplement growth of the export sector of the economy, see Raúl Prebisch, "El

and of beginning the stage of production of capital goods designed to diversify output. In these countries the domestic market appeared to be large enough to stimulate economic activity. It was assumed that the transfer of labor from sectors of low productivity—mainly in rural areas—into sectors of high productivity would broaden the market. Later, about 1955, a new element, income redistribution, was considered necessary by political economists to broaden the market and to attain development. With all these factors acting together it seemed certain that growth would be automatically generated by market forces.

Such a possibility, solidly supported by the postwar economic situation, was formulated as a theory in the most important studies on economic development written in Latin America. Previously, industrialization was viewed as just a supplementary resource for development based on the export of primary products. Until World War II, industrialization was accepted as a forced alternative during periods of world depression, but not as the key factor in development. During the fifties there occurred a drastic change in these views. Industrialization began to be looked on as a new phase in economic growth, which would follow export expansion and thus complete the cycle of development based on the export of primary products and also initiate self-sustained growth. Such growth was to be based on the stimulus of the domestic market and on the diversification of industrial output, which would lead to the creation of a domestic industry of capital goods.

Latin America would continue to be linked to the world market, to ensure buyers for its export products as well as to obtain foreign investment. Nevertheless, the expansion of the domestic market would assure continuing development.

_____

desarrollo económico de la América Latina y algunos de sus principales problemas," *Boletín Económico de América Latina,* 7 (1962): 1–24. The "import substitution" period or cycle is the designation of policies that encourage the local production of industrial goods that were formerly imported from abroad.

"Export industries" would still be needed to maintain "import capacity," but basically development would be determined by the domestic and not the foreign market.

There is no question but that at the beginning of the 1950s some of the conditions for this new phase in economic development in Latin America had been met, at least in countries like Argentina, Mexico, Chile, Colombia, and Brazil. Among these conditions were (1) a sufficiently large domestic market, created in the preceding century by the expansion of agricultural and mining economies whose products were exported to the world market but nevertheless required local investment and created some prosperity; (2) an industrial base that had evolved over the previous eighty years and which included light consumer-goods industries (foodstuffs, textiles, etc.) and in some cases the production of goods related to the export economy; (3) abundant foreign exchange derived from agricultural and mining output; (4) strong incentives to economic growth, especially in countries like Brazil and Colombia, thanks to the strengthening of the external sector during the second half of the 1950s; and (5) the existence of a satisfactory rate of domestic capital formation in such countries as Argentina.[2]

From an economic standpoint, therefore, it seemed that development policy should concentrate on two goals: the absorption of technology to diversify the structure of output and to increase productivity, and definition by the state of investment policies that would create the infrastructure needed for that diversification.[3] Favorable structural conditions and current prospects led to the belief, common among

2. For a discussion of the conditions for development in Argentina, see Benjamin Hopenhavn, "Estancamiento e inestabilidad: el caso argentino en la etapa de sustitución forzosa de importaciones," *El Trimestre Económico* (Mexico), no. 125 (January–March 1965), pp. 126–139.

3. The other alternative would have been to increase per capita income in primary production in order to offset the deterioration in the terms of trade. See Prebisch, *op. cit.*, especially p. 6.

economists, that development depended mainly on the ability of each country to take the policy decisions that its economic situation might require.

After the 1929 depression, even Latin American countries with a "liberal" economic tradition, like Argentina, began to strengthen the instruments of public power as a means to improve and regulate the export economy. The next step was to create public institutions to promote development along the new lines and to redefine goals and procedures used by the state officials entrusted with decision-making.

Strengthening and modernizing the state seemed so necessary a means of achieving an effective and efficient development policy that Latin American economists turned to the concept of a "political economy" to emphasize the political aspect of their proposals. The Latin American situation seemed to require a type of development concentrating on the nation-state. It seemed that domestic markets should be expanded and the centers of national decision-making so organized as to be sensitive to the development problems of their own countries.

After the 1950s the optimism based on the possibility of such a type of development began to wane. It is difficult to explain why the necessary measures were not taken to ensure continued development or why the measures taken were not effective. In some cases, the rate of economic growth was not sufficient to vitalize the more backward sectors of the economy, and the economy therefore could not absorb the pressure of population increase: it is well known that the demographic rate of growth is higher in depressed areas and among poor populations; with a low rate of investment, the offering of jobs can hardly meet the growing demand for them. The type of technology adopted by the most modern sectors used little labor and thus increased what seemed to be an overt incapacity to solve occupational demand through industrialization. The creation of new industrial sectors dismantled handicraft ones, destroying more jobs than creating new ones. It is true that the very dynamism of industrialization prevented depressions, and forecasts of catastrophy based on the capital-intensive type of industrialization (instead of a labor-intensive one) did not come about.

If economic conditions of the most prosperous countries of the area were conducive to development until the middle of the 1950s, was it that institutional and social conditions did not permit these favorable economic events to express themselves in a development policy? Or was the belief that development was possible itself mistaken?

In some countries like Brazil, events in the 1950s encouraged hope for self-sustained growth. Brazil's process of import substitution resulted in a capital goods sector. This sector not only assures more dynamism than the industrialization based on consumer goods—for it requires the use of sophisticated technology and has backward and forward linkage effects—but also implies that even in crisis periods it is extremely difficult to fall back from the technological level already attained. So, the steps ahead given by industrialization appeared to herald a new and irreversible stage in Brazilian development. However, the boom that reached its peak in the process of import substitution was followed in the 1960s by a period of relative stagnation that continued to hamper the Brazilian economy during almost all of that decade.[4]

Of the three most industrially advanced countries, only Mexico has managed to maintain a high rate of growth for a longer period. It must be recognized that Mexico's economic structure, especially the commodity spread of its export sector, differentiates it from other countries of Latin America. However, even in the Mexican case, bad income distribution

4. See "Auge y declinación del proceso de importaciones en el Brasil," *Boletín Económico de América Latina,* 9 (1964): 1–62. Nevertheless, the characteristics of the Brazilian economy would indicate that from an economic standpoint this stagnation is still within a "development" situation.

and the growing participation of foreign capital in the economy make it hard to tell what conditions are necessary in general for self-sustained growth beneficial to societies.

The economic forecasts made at the end of the 1940s and their underlying theory failed to explain the subsequent course of events. Argentina did not experience either the accelerated development or the qualitative changes that had been expected. Although Brazil found a temporary solution for its economic problems in the development surge of the 1950s, supported by short-term external financing, it went into a recession just when it appeared to have finally overcome the obstacles to development.[5] Mexico, after a difficult period of readjustment and profound transformations brought about by a nationalist policy, would seem to have realized its possibilities for expansion largely thanks to its integration into the world market through foreign investment and the diversification of its foreign trade, in which tourism plays an important role.

In view of the above, it is possible to generalize the question of why national economies as promising as Argentina's lacked the requisite vitality. To what extent may the very fact of the Mexican Revolution, which destroyed the balance of social forces, have been the fundamental factor in subsequent development? Could it not have been the play of Brazil's political and social forces during the ''development'' decade that was responsible for the initial impetus and also for the later loss of momentum in the process of development in Brazil in the early sixties?

Economic development in Latin America has frequently depended on favorable conditions for exports. It was precisely foreign trade that declined after the Korean War boom, accompanied by a steady deterioration in the terms of trade. To cope with emerging circumstances, the redefinition of the terms of international cooperation through programs of direct

---

5. Celso Furtado, *Desenvolvimento e subdesenvolvimento* (Rio de Janeiro: Editora Fundo de Cultura, 1961), especially chapter 5.

external financing of the public sector or a policy of price support have been suggested as supplementary requirements, but such measures were not effectively carried out.

These facts partly account for the slowdown of economic growth. The rate of increase in the gross product barely permitted reorganization of the economic system in a few countries. Neither the social nor the political system was reorganized in the hoped-for direction. This suggests that even though "traditional" society transformed its economic features, some of its old social sectors retained control of the system of power.[6] With the decline in the growth rate after the boom of the 1950s, the old problems of the hemisphere reappeared with new social protagonists, or with the same old ones in modern dress.

Nevertheless, it is not enough to replace the "economic" interpretation of development with "sociological" analysis. What is needed is an analysis that makes possible a broader and more sophisticated answer to the general question of how development is possible in the Latin American countries.

6. See for example ECLA (United Nations Economic Commission for Latin America), *El desarrollo social de América Latina en la postguerra* (Buenos Aires: Solar/Hachette, 1963), which advances the theory of the flexibility of traditional domination.

CHAPTER TWO

Comprehensive Analysis of Development

Development is itself a social process. To the economic assumption that underdevelopment leads to development through the creation of a dynamic domestic sector capable of generating both self-sustained growth and the transfer of the "decision-making center," some authors have added a sociological interpretation of the transition from traditional to modern societies.

Traditional and Modern Societies

It is argued that Latin American societies belong to a structural type generally called "traditional," which is giving way to another type of society called "modern."[1] It would appear that before becoming modern a society enters an intermediate, hybrid pattern called "structural dualism,"

1. This analytical approach stressing the passage from a traditional to a modern society is related specifically to Latin America

and that this pattern is characteristic of "developing" countries.[2]

This scheme is a reincarnation of the classical "community-society" dichotomy formulated by Tönnies. It is open to criticism from two points of view. On the one hand, the concepts of "traditional" and "modern" are neither broad enough to cover all existing social situations nor specific enough to distinguish the structures that define the ways of life of different societies. On the other hand, these concepts do not show how the different economic stages (for example, underdevelopment or development through exports or through import substitution, etc.) are linked to the various

---

by R. Redfield in *The Folk Culture of Yucatan* (Chicago: University of Chicago Press, 1940). B. Hoselitz later gives it a decidedly sociological orientation in *Sociological Factors in Economic Development* (Glencoe: Free Press, 1960) and applies it to Latin America in *Contribution to the First International Conference in Economic History: Stockholm, 1960* (The Hague: Mouton & Co., 1960). Gino Germani is possibly the Latin American who has best set forth this approach in, for example, his *Política y sociedad en una época de transición* (Buenos Aires: Paidós, 1962). It should be noted that Talcott Parsons, *The Social System* (Glencoe: Free Press, 1951), and Robert K. Merton, *Social Theory and Social Structure* (Glencoe: Free Press, 1949), have decisively influenced the formulation of this type of development analysis. Furthermore, Daniel Lerner, in *The Passing of Traditional Society: Modernizing the Middle East* (Glencoe: Free Press, 1958), states in more general terms—that is, not oriented toward the problem of development—the traditionalism and modernism approach in an analysis of the processes of social change. The psychological aspects of the passage from traditionalism to modernism are discussed by Everett Hagen, in *On the Theory of Social Change* (Homewood: Dorsey Press, 1962), and by David McClelland, in *The Achieving Society* (Princeton: Van Nostrand, 1961).

2. For the concept of structural dualism in this context, see Jacques Lambert, *Le Brésil: structure sociale et institutions politiques* (Paris: 1953), and from the viewpoint of an economist, Albert O. Hirschman, *The Strategy of Economic Development* (New Haven: Yale University Press, 1958).

types of social structure that are attributed to "traditional" and "modern" societies.

With this kind of characterization it continues to be impossible to explain the transition from one type of society to another. In fact, change in social structures, far from being only a cumulative process of incorporating new "variables," involves a series of relations among social groups, forces, and classes, through which some of them try to impose their domination over society.[3]

In purely economic terms, the degree of development of a production sector can be analyzed through a group of variables—the relation between the number of workers and capital, industrial output per added capital, and so forth—that reflect the process of structural diversification of the economy. Using this analysis as a base, the structure of society is deduced principally from the pattern of income distribution and the structure of employment. However, this strictly economic analysis can only be related to political and social development by looking beyond the social structure to its process of formation and to the social forces exerting pressure to maintain or change it.

Analyses that relate development to modern society and underdevelopment to traditional society are too simple. Development and modernization are not necessarily related just because domination in developed societies excludes "traditional groups." It may happen that a society modernizes its patterns of consumption, education, and so forth without a corresponding advance in development, if by development we understand less dependency and self-sustained growth based on the local capital accumulation and on the dynamism of the industrial sector.

3. See for example Peter Heintz, *Análisis contextual de los países latino-americanos* (Berkeley: mimeographed edition).

Social Change: External Models, Demonstration Effect, and Specific Situations

In almost all theories of modernization it is assumed that the course taken by political, social, and economic systems of Western Europe and the United States foretells the future for the underdeveloped countries. The "development process" would consist in completing and even reproducing the various stages that characterized the social transformation of these countries.[4] Therefore, the historical variations, the specificities of each situation of underdevelopment, have little value for this type of sociology.

It would be naive to assume that Latin America is in the nineteenth century while the developed countries are in the twentieth. More frequently, the underdeveloped countries are described as being "backward" in certain aspects of their structure although not in others. Thus, labor unions in countries like Brazil and Argentina became national and influenced decisions on wage levels during a phase that was abnormal by comparison with what had occurred in the countries of "early development." Accelerated urbanization in Latin America, which has come before industrialization, has helped to spread expectations and forms of political behavior that encourage greater participation of the masses in the power game before there is autonomous economic growth based on a domestic market. Such popular demands to share in the decisions affecting consumption are considered by many authors a "precocious" datum in the development process of Latin America.

It has been suggested that, because this level of participation is supposedly similar to that of the central countries,

4. See especially W. W. Rostow, *The Stage of Economic Growth, A Non-Communist Manifest* (Cambridge: Cambridge University Press, 1962); Wilbert Moore, *Economy and Society* (New York: Doubleday, 1955); Clark Kerr, et al., *Industrialism and Industrial Man* (Cambridge: Harvard University Press, 1960).

it might serve as a kind of bridge tending to approximate the social patterns and value orientations of the underdeveloped societies to those of the developed, modernizing them, even if not assuring similar levels of economic growth. This, broadly speaking, is what has come to be called the "demonstration effect": the modernization of consumption patterns, implying some degree of income improvement for urban population.

In an economic analysis, the "demonstration effect" assumes that the economy will be modernized through consumption and that ultimately modernization alters the production system in such a way that it may deviate from the "stages" of industrialization characteristic of advanced countries. But since investments depend to a large extent on domestic savings, the modernizing pressure of consumption can act also as a brake on development: it may stimulate the importation of consumer goods orienting the utilization of savings to the payment of external producers, as well as induce investment in sectors that are not basic to the economy.

On the other hand, the "demonstration effect" has not been thought of only in economic terms. Presumably, the pressures to modernize consumption are also pressures to change other aspects of human behavior—in the political and social areas—before diversification of the production system is completed. It should be stressed that the "demonstration effect" took place, at least until the sixties in the case of Latin America, because there was a minimum participation of the people in the political process. Sociological analysis should explain this measure of modernization to avoid simplistic interpretations that take "demonstration effect" by itself as "causal" explanation of the developing process. This kind of approach amounts to saying that the dynamism of underdeveloped societies derives from external factors and that the structural particularities in underdeveloped countries produce forms of development that are deviant cases when compared with classic stages of growth.

Rather than stressing the consequences of the "demonstration effect" or of other exogenous variables as a "modernizing factor" in the functioning of the economic system or in the behavior of social groups, it is important to study the historical-structural contexts in which such a process is generated since they reveal the very meaning of such modernization. We have therefore emphasized the specifics of the Latin American situation as principal conditioning factors in the development process. In this approach, the "demonstration effect" is incorporated into the analysis as a subordinate explanatory element. It is more basic for us to describe the relations among social groups at the national level, which of course also depend on linkages between the economic system and the international political blocs.

Structure and Process: Reciprocal Determination

To analyze development properly, we must consider in their totality the "historic specificities," both economic and social, underlying the development processes at the national and international levels. Within given structural situations, we must understand the conflict between social movements that "are set in motion" by social classes in developing societies. Our approach must examine not only structural conditions and the ideologies of the social movements, but also their relations and their reciprocal determination.

How can we link the economic and social components of development in an analysis of the behavior of social groups? First of all, every economic link is, by itself, a social link. Capital itself is the economic expression of a social relation; it requires the existence of a set of persons working by wage—selling its labor force—and another group owning machines and money to buy raw material and to pay wages and salaries. On the other hand, such an "economic" relation supposes not only exploitation—and thus social mechanisms to assure domination—but some degree of stability and recurrence in the relations of exploitation. Then this form of relation has a structure. Nevertheless, if structures already built appear as a mechanism that promotes the "natural" reinforcement of a given social order, they have in fact been built as a result of social struggles and are, in that sense, a historical product. Consequently, economic relations and the social structures on which they are based have to be studied as a process through which different classes try to sustain, preserve, or change interests rooted in social structures. Development results therefore from the interaction and struggles of social groups and classes that have specific ways of relating to each other. The social and political structure is modified insofar as new social classes and groups succeed in imposing their interests on or accommodating them to previous dominant classes in society.

Social change depends on historical alternatives. In the tensions between groups with divergent interests and directions, it finds the filter through which the purely economic influences have to pass.[5]

Our basic theoretical problem is how to determine what forms the structures of domination will adopt, because through these structures the dynamics of class relations may be understood. Political institutions at a given moment can only be fully understood in terms of the structures of domination because these express the class interests behind political organization. These structures also make it possible to follow the process of change at the political-institutional level. Significant historical changes in the process of Latin American development have always been accompanied, if not by a radical alteration of the structure of domination, at least by the adoption of new forms of relations and, consequently, of conflict between classes and groups. In that sense, the oligarchical period characteristic of the export economy drive

5. For an analysis of this point of view, see F. H. Cardoso, *Empresário industrial e desenvolvimento econômico no Brasil* (São Paulo: Difusão Europeia do Livro, 1964), chapters 1 and 2.

was replaced, for instance, by the "populist" period of soaring industrialization oriented toward internal markets. In the case of economically dependent countries, the explanation of structures of domination involves establishing the links that may exist between internal and external determinants. These links should not be understood in terms of a mechanical and immediate determination of the internal by the external: it is important to delineate the interconnections between these two levels, suggesting the ways through which external factors are interwoven with internal ones.

The concept of dependence tries to give meaning to a series of events and situations that occur together, and to make empirical situations understandable in terms of the way internal and external structural components are linked. In this approach, the external is also expressed as a particular type of relation between social groups and classes within the underdeveloped nations. For this reason, it is worth focusing the analysis of dependence on its internal manifestations.

Because the purpose of this essay is to explain the economic processes as social processes, it is necessary to find a theoretical point of intersection where economic power is pressed as domination, that is to say, as politics. An economic class or group tries to establish through the political process a system of social relations that permits it to impose on the entire society a social form of production akin to its own interests; or at least it tries to establish alliances or to control the other groups or classes in order to develop an economic order consistent with its interests and objectives. The modes of economic relations, in turn, set the limits of political action.

Thus the topics to be dealt with are the economic factors conditioning the world market; the structure of the national production system and the kind of linkage it has developed with the external market; the historical-structural shape of such societies, with their ways of assigning and maintaining power; and above all, the political-social movements and processes that exert pressure toward change, and their respective orientations and objectives. Direct analysis of the main socio-political processes in underdeveloped or developing societies is an immense and limitless task. Nevertheless, there are certain topics that, although of a particular character, throw light on the overall situation. In particular, it is illuminating to look for the points where the economic system intersects with the social system, which will indicate the links and dynamics that affect the possibility of development.

By and large, the problems of social control of production and consumption are the axis of a sociological analysis of development viewed from this perspective. The sociological interpretation of economic change requires analysis of tensions between social groups which reveal what supports the economic and political structure.

Although it is now fashionable to analyze "decision-making mechanisms" from this angle, no sociological view of the problem of development can be reduced to this approach, because it misses the point that is crucial for us: social forces and structural determinants behind political processes. Development always alters the social system of domination as it changes the organization of production and consumption. It cannot be reduced to changes at the institutional level or to the analysis of actors' value orientations. This view of the problem encourages us to analyze the political behavior of social classes that maintain control at the structural level and those that oppose such control. Moreover, it moves us to consider the value orientations that give the action its framework of reference, not at the individual level, but at the cultural one, as ideologies.

Underdevelopment, Periphery, and Dependence

The historical specificity of the situation of underdevelopment derives from the relation between "peripheral" and "central" societies. Underdeveloped countries must be distinguished from those without development: the latter are economies and peoples—fast disappearing—that do not have market relations with the industrialized countries. As for underdevelopment, in some situations the linkage between the peripheral economies and the world market can be described as "colonial," whereas in others the peripheral economies belong to "national societies." In the latter case some peripheral countries already had a national society when they formed links with the more developed dominant centers, while others were colonies that became nations but without any change in their situation of underdevelopment.

In any event, the situation of underdevelopment came about when commercial capitalism and then industrial capitalism expanded and linked to the world market nonindustrial economies that went on to occupy different positions in the overall structure of the capitalist system. Thus, there exists among the developed and underdeveloped economies a difference, not only of the stage or the state of the production system, but also of function or position within the international economic structure of production and distribution: some produce industrial goods; others, raw material. This requires a definite structure of relations of domination to assure an international trade based on merchandise produced at unequal levels of technology and cost of labor force.

The concept of underdevelopment, as it is usually employed, refers to a type of economic system with a predominant primary sector, a high concentration of income, little diversification in its production system, and above all, an external market far outweighing the internal. This concept will not suffice.

Understanding the historicity of the underdevelopment situation requires more than just an indication of the structural characteristics of underdeveloped economies. It is necessary to analyze how the underdeveloped economies were linked historically to the world market and how internal social groups defined the outward-directed relations implicit in underdevelopment. Dependence on the sociopolitical level also began historically with the expansion of the economies of the early capitalist countries. In extreme cases of dependence, decisions affecting the production or consumption of a given economy are taken in terms of the growth and interests of the developed economies; a typical example is the economy based on a colonial enclave.

The foregoing argument suggests that the distinction between "central" and "peripheral" economies has greater social significance than that between developed and underdeveloped economies. The former can incorporate immediately the idea of unequal positions and functions within the same structure of overall production. Nonetheless, it would not be sufficient or correct to replace the concepts of development and underdevelopment with those of a central and a peripheral economy, or—as if it were a synthesis of both—with those of an autonomous and a dependent economy. These concepts differ as much in their dimensions as in their theoretical meaning. The idea of dependence refers to the conditions under which alone the economic and political system can exist and function in its connections with the world productive structure. The idea of underdevelopment refers to the degree of diversification of the production system without emphasizing the patterns of control of decisions on production and consumption, whether internal (socialism, capitalism, etc.) or external (colonialism, periphery of the world market, etc.). The ideas of "center" and "periphery" stress the functions that underdeveloped economies perform in the world market, but overlook the socio-political factors involved in the situation of dependence.

A society can undergo profound changes in its production system without the creation of fully autonomous decision-making centers. Such was the case when Argentina and Brazil ended the process of import substitution and began the production of capital goods. They had attained a degree of economic maturity, even—as happened to some extent in Argentina—in income distribution. In spite of that, not only is its industrial sector controlled from abroad, but it plays a complementary and subordinated role from the standpoint of the international capitalist system. A national society can achieve a certain autonomy of decision without thereby having a production system and an income distribution comparable to those in the central developed countries or even in some peripheral developing countries. This can occur, for example, when a country breaks its ties with a given system of domination without incorporating itself totally into another (Yugoslavia, China, Algiers, Egypt, Cuba, and even Revolutionary Mexico).

Since there need not be an immediate connection between the diversification of the economic system and the formation of autonomous decision-making centers, analyses should define not only the degree of economic diversification and social differentiation reached by countries that are being integrated into the world market, but also the manner in which this integration was achieved historically. Such an approach calls for great caution in interpreting how the economy of Latin America has developed and its society has been modernized.

Various authors have emphasized development as an "unforeseen result" in Latin America. Some countries, for example, when planning the defense of their principal export product, carried out a currency devaluation policy that had the indirect and not altogether intended consequence of creating favorable conditions for industrial growth. Nevertheless, it would be difficult to claim that the economic diversification achieved in this way—during market fluctuations and without a program for increasing autonomy and changing class relations—can alone substantively alter the relations of dependence. The political sphere of social behavior necessarily influences the form of the development process.

Thus, in a global interpretation of development, arguments based solely on market incentives and reactions do not suffice to explain industrialization and the economic process. Such incentives or mechanisms to defend the economy can only begin an industrialization process; its continuation requires changes favorable to development in the international market and, still more essential, elements favorable to a broader measure of autonomy within the socio-political game of the developing countries.

What we seek are the characteristics of the national societies that express relations with the outside. The internal socio-political factors—linked naturally to the dynamic of the hegemonic centers—are precisely the ones that may produce policies taking advantage of the "new conditions" or new opportunities for economic growth. Similarly, it is the internal forces that give socio-political scope to the "spontaneous" diversification of the economic system. For example, the traditional dominant groups initially may oppose handing over their power of control to the new social groups that appear with industrialization, but they also may bargain with them, thereby altering the social and political consequences of development. National economic groups are connected with external groups in different ways and with different consequences before and after the development process begins. Moreover, the internal system of political alliances is often modified by international alliances.

We cannot accurately discuss the development process just from a strictly economic angle when our stated objective is to understand the formation of the national economies. Nor, for purposes of description, is it enough to analyze the behavior of variables—such as productivity, savings, and income rates, and consumption and employment functions— since these depend on structural factors and the historical process of change.

In the "colonial enclave" situation, the political subordination of the colony highlights the fact that the economic system is directly bound to the political system. On the other hand, when development takes place in "national states," the economic aspect becomes more visible; the political and social hegemony becomes less visible, but continues to influence whatever opportunities for development may appear in the market.

If it is accepted that market influences by themselves neither explain development nor guarantee its continuity or direction, then the behavior of social groups and institutions becomes crucial to the analysis of development.

"National Underdevelopment"

In situations of extreme colonial dependency local history is almost reduced to a reflection of what happens in a metropolis. However, the decision by local forces to rebel against colonialism and to create a nation implies an attempt to influence local history according to local values and interests. Economic links with external markets still impose limits to decisions and actions even after independence. The contradiction between the attempt to cope with the market situation in a politically autonomous way and the de facto situation of dependency characterizes what is the specific ambiguity of nations where political sovereignty is expressed by the new state and where economic subordination is reinforced by the international division of labor and by the economic control exerted by former or new imperialist centers. From a sociological viewpoint, here is perhaps the core of the problem of national development in Latin America.

"National underdevelopment" is a situation of objective economic subordination to outside nations and enterprises and, at the same time, of partial political attempts to cope with "national interests" through the state and social movements that try to preserve political autonomy. Ideological components play some role in the perception of what "national interest" means, as well as in the rationalization about the possibility of the existence of nation-states that have submitted to foreign interests and pressures.

One of the aims of comprehensive analyses of the national development process is to determine the links between social groups that in their behavior actually tie together the economic and political spheres. Insofar as, by definition, links of economic dependency imply a relationship between local and external classes, states, and enterprises, the analyses of local social and political groups must include the connections with international partners. Some local classes or groups sustain dependency ties, enforcing foreign economic and political interests. Others are opposed to the maintenance of a given pattern of dependency. Dependence thus finds not only internal "expression," but also its true character as implying a situation that structurally entails a link with the outside in such a way that what happens "internally" in a dependent country cannot be fully explained without taking into consideration the links that internal social groups have with external ones. Dependence should no longer be considered an "external variable"; its analysis should be based on the relations between the different social classes within the dependent nations themselves.

This analysis does away with the idea that class relations in dependent countries are like those of the central countries during their early development. At the beginning of the development process in the central countries, market forces generally act as arbiter in the conflict of interests between the dominant groups. Thus, economic rationality, measured in money, was made a norm of society; and consumption and investment were limited by the growth of the economic system. Expansion of the system was due to a dynamic group that controlled investment decisions and imposed upon the entire society an orientation based on its own interests. The rising economic class possessed efficiency and consensus in capitalistic terms.

It was believed that the ruling groups expressed the general interest and that the market functioned adequately as a mechanism to satisfy general and particular interests. Other groups that exerted pressure in order to share in the fruits of "progress" and in decision-making were ignored. Only long after the initial stage of industrialization did the popular classes participate politically and socially in the industrial societies.[6]

6. See Alain Touraine, "Industrialisation et conscience ouvrière a São Paulo," *Sociologie du Travail* (April 1961).

The national economies in the countries of "early growth" succeeded in part because they were consolidated at the same time that the world market expanded, so that these countries came to occupy the leading positions in the system of international domination. From this scheme it is evident that "early development," although a very broad and imprecise term, is significantly different from what has occurred in Latin America.

It has been assumed that the peripheral countries would have to repeat the evolution of the economies of the central countries in order to achieve development. But it is clear that from its beginning the capitalist process implied an unequal relation between the central and the peripheral economies. Many "underdeveloped" economies—as is the case of the Latin American—were incorporated into the capitalist system as colonies and later as national states, and they have stayed in the capitalist system throughout their history. They remain, however, peripheral economies with particular historical paths when compared with central capitalist economies.

Capitalism should be studied in the hope, not of finding how its history may repeat at a later date in the peripheral countries, but of learning how the relation between peripheral and central was produced. Although it is possible to distinguish in the economic history of Latin America the periods of mercantile, industrial, and financial capitalism, it is important for us to make clear what the relation of dependence meant in each of these phases. It would be senseless to seek how far or how close Latin American economies are from "mercantilism," "industrialism," or "finance" forms of capitalism. They belong to the same international capitalistic system as central economies do. Consequently the history of central capitalism is, at the same time, the history of peripheral capitalism. But specific links between dependent and central economies could have been different in each of the above periods. The same can be argued vis-à-vis analyses about competitive or monopolistic trends in the development of capitalism and its effects on peripheral economies.

During these different phases of the capitalist process, the Latin American countries depended on various countries that acted as centers and whose economic structures influenced the nature of the dependence. For example, Great Britain's economic expansion required some measure of development in the peripheral economies, since it relied on them to supply raw materials. Furthermore, these same economies were part of the market for its manufactured products. It was therefore necessary for Latin American production to achieve a certain degree of growth and modernization. The United States economy, on the other hand, had its own natural resources as well as a domestic market that permitted it a more autonomous development in respect of the peripheral economies; in some cases it even competed with the countries producing raw materials. The relation of dependence thus came to denote control of the development of other economies both in the production of raw materials and in the possible formation of other economic centers. The vitalizing role of the United States in the Latin American economies was therefore less important (prior to the formation of the present multinationals) than the role performed by English capitalism.

The developing countries are by no means repeating the history of the developed countries. Historical conditions are different. When the world market was created along with development, it was thanks to the action of the "bourgeoisie conquérante." Now, development is undertaken when capitalist market relations already exist between both groups of countries and when the world market is divided between the capitalist and socialist worlds. What at first glance may appear to be deviant forms of the classic development pattern are simply not. When we recognize this, the present socio-economic system in dependent countries may become understandable.

Types of Linkage Between the National Economies and the Market

The rupture of what historians call the "colonial pact" and the early expansion of European industrial capitalism were the dominant historical features in the formation of the "new nations" in the nineteenth century. Expansion of the central industrialized economies, first of England and later of the United States, was carried out in the presence of the economic and social systems established by the preceding colonial expansion. Conversely, peripheral national economies fed into the different phases of the capitalist process. The development of a nation exporting a widely consumed product would differ according to whether the phase of capitalism was predominantly competitive or predominantly monopolistic. In the first case, chances are more favorable for local producers to find a place in the market. In the latter case, international monopolies usually try to control local production. In the same way, a country whose economy had been that of a colony of settlement, largely self-sufficient and using abundant labor, would differ from an exploitation colony that was more strictly exploited from the outside: after independence, the former could more easily organize an internal political-administrative apparatus to promote and carry out a "national policy." Furthermore, the physical foundation of a country's economy—for example, the type and possibilities of land occupation or the type of available mineral wealth—would influence the nature of its link with the world market after the period of national formation.

When Latin America emerged from its colonial dependence and entered a period of dependence on Great Britain, Britain sought support from national producers of export commodities who, because of the growth of their economic base—already under way in the colonial situation—could effect a new accommodation with emergent dominant forces at world level. Thanks to this they gained, if not absolute control, at least a privileged position in local structures of power.

In the passage from British to United States hegemony, new factors came into play: growth of the exporting groups was accompanied by a significant growth of the urban sectors of the economies, especially industry. Although the new form of dependence had explanations outside the nation—it re-flects the expansion of industrial corporations at the world level—internal class relations made it possible and gave it shape. The growth of the dependent economic system within the nation was determined, within limits, by the capacity that the internal systems of alliance between classes and groups and the hegemonic position of these alliances over society had to assure economic expansion. The pressure of the masses in recent years to incorporate themselves into the political system has spurred the dynamism of the prevailing economic form: dominant groups have expanded internal markets, and thus it is possible for them to absorb social pressures from below.

During this "nationalist-populist" period, the popular classes often allied with the new economically dominant groups tried to impose their participation and came into con-flict with the systems of alliance existing among landlords and exporting sectors of the earlier situation.

The industrial group at first appeared in a marginal situation. Nevertheless, it was the only group in the new urban sectors that possessed a real economic base. As the one group that could absorb the urban popular sectors in a pro-ductive way, it was strategically situated to establish terms of alliance or compromise with the rest of the social system. This also accounts for its importance in the period following the crisis of the agro-export system.

Toward a Comprehensive Analysis of Development

There is no doubt that an analysis is needed to redefine, within the context of development, the meaning and func-tions of social classes and of the alliances they establish to maintain a structure of power and to generate social change and economic growth.

In developing but dependent countries, social structures reflect the double edge of the economic system: its external links and internal roots. Thus, social dynamics and social conflicts usually express both kinds of interests and pressures, those that derive from external influences and those that are national. Yet, as we stressed before, foreign interests have internal expression through the action of groups and persons who represent them or have advantages in their presence. It is not necessarily foreign interests that are represented or sustained by "modernizing elites." "Traditional" groups— for instance, large landlords—are often the main sustaining force for foreign interests. On the other hand, after the industrialization of peripheral economies under the control of multinational corporations, previous industrializing spurts have gained continuity and have considerably expanded. This implies the growth of urban working classes, as well as the diversification of social stratification. New middle-class groups—technicians, private and public employers, people devoted to the service sector, professionals, and so forth— have gained strength in society. The strong participation of the state in the economic process of growth has enlarged the participation of bureaucracies and of the military in Latin American societies. All together these processes show the complexity of the situation of underdevelopment. It gives rise to activities of social groups corresponding to the patterns of "industrialized mass societies"—as in the case of urban patterns of mass consumption vis-à-vis mass media influence on mass behavior—and at same time to others in which social norms typical of "class situations" prevail. The latter can be seen in the style of political confrontation in crises situations, as well as in the shape and functions of workers unions. Corporatist components of the political system indeed redefine class behavior, as is notorious in the case of unions under authoritarian regimes in Latin America. Sometimes even "state situations" (in the Weberian sense) have importance in the understanding of conflicts and accommodations that prevail: "traditional" sectors of middle and upper classes protect themselves through mechanisms of social identification—clubs, professional associations, and so forth— that are based not on direct economic or market interests but on specific forms of socialization and defense of privileges based on degrees of education, family origin, and shared values.

If we admit that those factors of differentiation and complexity are intermixed with the above mentioned multiple links with external societies and economic interests, it is not difficult to see the reasons why analyses of dependency need theoretical efforts to stress specificities.

The social and economic transformations that alter the internal and external aspects of the underdeveloped and dependent societies are actually political processes that, in present historical conditions, do not always favor national development. Our analysis of social development always assumes the possibility of stagnation and heteronomy. To determine the possibilities of success, it is necessary to analyze not only structure but also the action of social forces—both those that tend to maintain the status quo and those that exert pressure for social change—as well as the "value orientations" or ideologies that are associated with social actions and movements. Since these forces are interrelated and express a market situation with various possibilities of growth, analysis is complete only when the economic and the social have their reciprocal determinations defined at the internal and external levels.

CHAPTER THREE

The Period of "Outward Expansion"

The development and consolidation of the Latin American national states have depended on how successful local social classes have been in participating in the production process and in setting up institutional controls to ensure that participation. Creation of the national states and control of the local economies together establish a "legitimate order" based on the associated interests of the economically oriented classes. This order commands the consent of classes, groups, and communities excluded from the dominant nucleus.

The production system was the material foundation of the economic gains of the groups and classes that controlled output. By itself, or by the changes produced in it by the world market, it could not guarantee an automatic transformation of the system of power and a consequent democratization of the social structures. After the emergence of the independent national states, the different relations between the economic system and the system of power gave rise to different possibilities of development and autonomy in the Latin American countries according to their individual situations.

Thus, the present situations cannot be understood without an analysis, however brief, of the historical situations that explain how the Latin American nations fit into the world system of power and the periphery of the international economy.

Rupture of the Colonial Pact, 1810–1825

Events in Europe at the end of the eighteenth century changed the relations between Portugal and Spain and their American colonies.[1] Because of fraud and contraband, Spain had been continually losing profits from the trade it tried to monopolize. At the same time, it had made several attempts to strengthen the administrative and military structures of domination, which almost always resulted in higher taxes. The administrative reforms of the last decades of the eighteenth century provoked a series of uprisings in the colonies, each with its individual features, but in general to protest against the heavier tax burden. Together with attempts at greater control, Spain instituted commercial reforms that ended the monopoly of Cadiz and promoted trade between ports, although this did not necessarily benefit local merchants. On the contrary, merchants from the Iberian peninsula, many of them connected with the large centers of Cadiz and Barcelona, took over. As historians have observed, the ascendancy of Buenos Aires over Lima or of Veracruz over

1. Almost all the information in this chapter is based on the excellent book by Tulio Halperín Donghi, *Historia contemporánea de América Latina* (Madrid: Alianza Editorial, 1969).

Mexico meant in the former case that the local merchants of Lima were displaced by the new Iberian merchants of Buenos Aires.

From 1795 on, Spanish power continued to decline. The war with Great Britain, which ended with British supremacy in the Atlantic, made it difficult for Spain to maintain not only its trade monopoly but also its military and administrative authority. Measures to cope with the situation were directed toward establishing trade relations with neutral countries and foreign colonies or toward intensifying trade among the colonies. The advances of modern capitalism had placed Spain in the role of intermediary between the colonies and the new industrial Europe. As a result of these political vicissitudes, merchants and especially producers in Latin America came to view colonial relations as an obstacle to be surmounted. They wanted to establish direct links with Great Britain, the new trade metropolis, to expand the market for their products, and to obtain a higher price for them by eliminating intermediaries. In short, they wanted a trade policy dictated by the colonies themselves.

To the problems in trade relations were added problems in the power relations of administration. By creating new viceroyalties and captaincies-general as well as a completely new system of *intendencias,* the Bourbon reform stirred up disputes over jurisdiction. The purpose of the Spanish crown was to establish an administration loyal to its interests, but this clashed with the power of local groups. Demands for greater autonomy were expressed in struggles between Iberians and *criollos.* To safeguard their interests, the metropolitan powers preferred to appoint Iberians to high positions in the administration, army, and church, thereby intensifying rivalries. For the criollos almost all the administrative body— viceroys, *intendentes,* and so forth—represented the power of Spain and Portugal imposed on the local upper classes. In its early stages, the Independence movement sought above all to replace those holding political power with members of the local oligarchies.

The predominance of Iberian merchants in local centers only added tensions to the rivalry between natives and Iberians. Even those who had benefited from the shift toward intracolonial trade were hostile to the newly rich merchants.

The events following upon the Napoleonic invasion of Spain were responsible for the first stirrings of unrest, which were expressed legitimately and pacifically. After the monarchy was toppled and seemed unlikely to be restored, wealthy and influential merchants and landlords in the colonies saw themselves as the rightful heirs. The *cabildos,* the initiators of liberation, laid claim to the continuity of legitimate power; but accumulated tensions hindered a peaceful transition. The criollos were prepared not only to seize greater autonomy but to change power relations in their favor. The Iberians detected a note of vengeance in this purpose: their continued rule in the colonies seemed identified with that of the monarchy. Civil war between the upper sectors was inevitable. The Iberians, functionaries, ecclesiastics, and military men used their power against the insurgents. The warring groups also tried to mobilize other sectors, and a struggle that at first appeared to be limited to a few small groups soon engulfed all. In some countries, especially Peru and Mexico, the widening of the conflict determined how Independence would come about.

In Peru, in the last two decades of the eighteenth century, there had been serious conflicts known as the "war of castes." In Lower Peru, the Indians had rebelled against the whites and mestizos; in Upper Peru (today Bolivia), they had been allied with the mestizos against the whites. Broadening of the conflicts between the criollo and Iberian elites in this context boded ill for elites of any sort. During the Independence period, an expeditionary force sent from Buenos Aires to conquer Upper Peru tried to enlist support of the Indians by freeing them from payment of tribute and declaring them absolutely equal. Although this measure was not wholly successful, the earlier experience with indigenous uprisings drove the criollos to unite with the cause of the monarchy, or at least not to oppose it very actively. Criollo hegemony was too risky, when a more solid "white" hegemony would be guaranteed by the "colonial order." Thus for a long time, Peru would be a bastion of defense of the Spanish crown.

Similarly, the mestizo and Indian problem lent special features to the Independence movement in Mexico. The rebellion there had its beginnings in a protest by these groups. In September 1810 the village priest, Father Hidalgo, incited the populace to revolt with these rallying cries: "for Independence, for the King, for religion, for the Indian Virgin of Guadalupe, and down with the Spaniards." The rebels were joined by the peasants who worked on haciendas and later by those who worked in mines. After Hidalgo's rebellion had been crushed, Morelos took up the struggle in 1812 with a program for independence, equality of classes, and division of large landed estates. This last was because the uprising was centered in the sugar-growing region where plantations had displaced the subsistence economies and created serious problems. As in Peru, the outbreaks led to unification of the Iberian and criollo elites, whose main interest was to defend the order against a dangerous revolution.

Even in countries where the presence of Indian or mestizo sectors did not endanger the upper-class groups, the conflicts generated by the rebellion were important. In Colombia and Venezuela, for example, these conflicts made it extremely difficult subsequently to organize the new state. The Church strongly resisted the process of transformation, the slave-owners on the Venezuelan coast felt threatened by the new republic's avowed intentions to emancipate the Negro, and large merchants and small craftsmen both feared a free-trade policy that might eliminate them under the pressure of English competition.

It is often repeated that, because the exploiting classes continued and in some cases even gained strength, nothing changed with the wars of Independence. But the wars, conflicts, and alliances had a marked influence on the subsequent course of events. Although the emancipation of the Indians in Upper Peru may not have had much practical significance, attention was drawn to sectors that in the colonial structure had been at the bottom of the scale, as well as to the mulattos and Negroes of Venezuela, and to the popular masses led by Güemes, himself an aristocrat, in Salta, Argentina. Present-day scholars point out that the Independence movement signified in many places a process of social mobility. The transformation of rebellion into a war—which lasted fifteen years—required the creation of real armies, where the officers may have been from the upper classes, but the soldiers and many of the noncommissioned officers were recruited from the lower classes. Paradoxically, this mobility was especially notable in the royalist armies, where officers of criollo origin occupied high ranks.

As one of the principal motives of the Independence movement was to find a new link with the outside, the countries that were to replace Spain and Portugal could not remain indifferent.

With the signing of the Peace of Ghent in 1814, the United States emerged from its second war of independence, but was not yet prepared to give official support to the Independence forces of the Latin American colonies. Nevertheless, its policy of neutrality made it increasingly easy for the rebels to acquire arms and vessels.

England, since the time of Hawkins, had been aware of the conflict between the interests of the inhabitants of the Spanish colonies and the crown. But it was only after the North American revolution was done with that England began to try to define a policy toward that part of the world. This policy could not be very consistent. In its attempts at direct intervention, such as the landing of troops in Buenos Aires in 1806, England risked reinforcing the alliance between Spain and France, which did not suit English aims in Europe. Later, in 1808, Spain became an ally of England against Napoleon, which imposed certain obligations on England to respect the colonial interests of the former country.

After the defeat of Napoleon and the Restoration in Spain, England felt less constrained. Although it did not come out in favor of Independence, together with the United

States it did facilitate the purchase of arms by the rebels and permit volunteers to join contingents such as the British Legion in Bolivar's army. This attitude toward Latin America was consistent with England's policy in Europe, where England opposed the designs of the Holy Alliance and particularly those of Spain and Russia. There is therefore some reason to believe that England, through its foreign secretary, Canning, and his representatives abroad, may have influenced the drawing up of the Monroe Doctrine in 1823. English policy appeared also to take into account the lessons learned from the political revolutions that toward the end of the eighteenth century had swept both Europe and America: that it was no longer practical to solve the problems of expansion by force.

The wars of Independence had been waged to achieve a political order and a different "pact" with the new metropolis. The way in which the latter evolved economically would put its stamp on Latin America.

At the end of the eighteenth and the beginning of the nineteenth centuries, there was a change in the policy of Great Britain owing to expansion of its industrial output. Great Britain wanted not only to ensure itself a supply of colonial products but also to gain access to larger markets. It therefore abandoned the complicated system of factories and mercantile establishments based on treaties in order to contract directly with the markets for rapid sale of its merchandise. At the moment of Latin America's Independence, Great Britain was more interested in exporting than in importing.

After Independence, the problem of national organization in Latin America consisted in keeping local control of an export-oriented production system while creating a system of internal political alliance that would permit the group that maintained relations with the outside (the world market and the national states of the central countries) a minimum of internal power to preserve stability and represent the economic domination of the export-oriented production sector.

Formation of the National State, 1825–1850

Restructuring the political order, once Independence was completed, involved dealing with the aftermath of years of war. Violence had spread and come to dominate every moment of daily life. Internal order could be maintained only through growing militarization; the armies and armed groups that had been mobilized for war remained and sometimes were expanded because of the continued violence. The expense of supporting them was a drain on national treasuries. It often happened that the chiefs of the armed groups broke away from the authority they were originally supposed to guarantee. In Mexico, the Independence armies had comprised a large number of officers whom nobody dared to discharge.

The problem of militarization and the emergence of *caudillos* affected various countries of Latin America for many years. During wartime, the regular army was mobile, and in several countries such as Argentina, Venezuela, Colombia, and Chile it was even employed outside national borders. To preserve local order, the power structure of the region often organized a militia. The caudillos of these militias came to express the demands and protests that many times were directed against the authority of the regular army. Regional demands supported by these armed bodies went so far as declarations of autonomy.

It has already been noted that war began a process of mobility that brought into prominence traditionally neglected groups. The army, which was the channel of this mobility, also served to brake the process before it could create difficulties for the dominant groups. Although militarization had its drawbacks, it was accepted as a guarantee of a relative and necessary order.

Besides soldiers, war left in its wake the destruction of a large part of the economy. The armies could be financed only by using up accumulated wealth. This wealth, which was in the hands of the urban oligarchies, in the treasures of churches and monasteries, and in the funds collected by the merchant guilds, was confiscated from royalties and patriots alike and consumed in the struggle. Furthermore, since the armies lived off the land, livestock and cereal crops were decimated.

It has been pointed out that Independence failed to change the real condition of the Indian masses, and that in some countries even their legal conditions did not change. This was not necessarily true of the free mulattos, the mestizos, and other marginal groups in Spanish America. In rural areas where some type of free work existed or in urban centers, these groups managed to take advantage of the revolutionary process. Moreover, one of the institutions most affected was slavery. Although Abolition was postponed by such measures as the Law of the Free Womb* and the prohibition of slave trade, war itself had compelled the emancipation of large groups, for example, the Negroes who fought in the Venezuelan war. The civil wars subsequently broadened this phenomenon because slaves became necessary as soldiers. The discipline of slave labor was profoundly altered, as could be seen on the Peruvian coast where productivity dropped dramatically.

War had affected rural society less than urban. Regional landholders retained their power, not only because they had at their service the militias that had been organized to preserve local order, but because a greater number of the rural population was under arms.

To help raise consumption in the war-damaged economy, power was restored to the landholders, usually by assuring them an adequate supply of labor. Even Artigas, the most "revolutionary" of the caudillos of the east bank of the River Plate, proclaimed that all people who did not own land had to prove that they were employed by someone. To the en-

---

*Translator's note: all children born of slave parents would thenceforth be free.

hanced power of the landholders was added that of the former generals and commanders, now transformed into *hacendados*. In Venezuela, these were the ones who would largely compose the ruling class of the conservative republic. The pre-Independence balance of power between urban and rural elites changed to favor the latter.

This change also indicated a breakdown in the institutions that had been of primary concern in the colonial period. The urban criollo groups had been eager to dislodge the Iberians from their privileged positions in the institutions of power; but with the rebellion, these institutions lost much of their significance and prestige. In addition, local merchants were gradually being displaced by foreign competition, so that the urban elites had to be satisfied with a subordinate incorporation into the new political and social order. In most cases, the axis of power would be for a long time the military forces.

If conditions for establishing relations among classes and groups were far from those imagined at the start of the Independence movement, neither were conditions for establishing new ties with the outside as positive as had been expected. In the first half of the nineteenth century, Great Britain and then Europe were bent upon meeting the demands for capital made by the "railroad era" both on the continent and in the United States. For this reason, there was no substantial capital investment from Great Britain or Europe in newly independent Latin America. This did not mean that there was not trade; on the contrary, Great Britain made every effort to maintain active trade with Latin America in order to accumulate capital for investment in the aforementioned enterprises. Great Britain was interested mostly in selling its industrial products on the Latin American market. It came to dominate local mercantile channels. Free trade did not prove to be very beneficial: with the breakdown of the old monopolies, international competition often had an adverse effect. In the former ex-Viceroyalty of the River Plate, textiles from Great Britain, sugar from Brazil, flour from the United

States, and wine and spirits from Europe and the Caribbean flowed into the markets of Buenos Aires to the detriment of local production, including cereals.

Special mention should be made of the fate of local merchants. Already weakened by the struggle for supremacy between Iberians and criollos, they had been ruined financially by forced loans that amounted to confiscation, and they had no means of defending themselves against their European competitors. They had wanted to break away from traditional trade links into channels that they would develop. International trade was now controlled by Great Britain from its center in London and, after 1820, in Liverpool. It was obvious that merchants had been irrevocably displaced.

To gain strength and improve trade links with the outside was a very difficult task in the first half of the nineteenth century. Some areas of Latin America maintained or even advanced the development they had reached by the end of the colonial period; others came to a standstill, and many regressed.

Venezuela, where the wars of Independence had been savage, nevertheless linked its agriculture to the world market and surpassed levels attained during the colonial period. The River Plate, which had been torn by civil wars, struggles among caudillos, and international conflicts, could base a favorable economic structure on its livestock production.

At the other extreme, Bolivia, Peru, and especially Mexico stagnated and even declined. Mining, which had been their most important source of revenue, was hard hit by the rebellion. Furthermore, mines could not be put back into operation without vast amounts of capital. Output of Mexican silver fell to only half that of the colonial period. In Central America, the same problems of lack of capital and absence of markets meant stagnation in spite of the enormous extensions of land owned by the hacendados. The exception was the central plateau of Costa Rica, where expansion of coffee production improved prospects for the export economy.

Economic Difficulties and Political Instability

FOREIGN INTERVENTION—MEXICO

The Mexican mining economy had been almost totally destroyed by the years of war, its installations damaged and, in 1821, many of its mines flooded. The capital needed for reconstruction had either been used to finance the war or transferred to Spain. The expansion of Mexican mining in the second half of the eighteenth century had been made possible by reinvestment and a steady inflow of new capital; now no capital could be obtained even for repairs and replacement. Because of the country's impoverishment, the government in 1823 was always in search of loans. Neither the money it borrowed in the London market, nor revenue from customs, taxes, and monopolies covered its expenditures. Having become creditors of the state, Great Britain, in competition with the United States, maneuvered for positions to control trade and other activities. Political life was divided between conservatives and liberals. The conservatives, known as the Escoceses because they banded together in a Scottish Masonic lodge, had close ties with the British minister in Mexico. The liberals and federalists belonged to a lodge that was an offshoot of one in New York (hence their name, Yorkinos) and they were advised by the United States minister.

Alongside these groups was the army, which played a far from subordinate role as keeper of domestic order. Its influence was enhanced by the disproportionate number of officers it had inherited from the Independence wars. The conservatives, who had triumphed over the liberals and who still remembered the uprisings led by Hidalgo and Morelos, saw in the army a safeguard against popular movements and therefore were prepared to grant it not only authority but also a large share in Mexico's revenues.

International problems involved more than just unwarranted interference in domestic politics. Border tensions erupted into a war with Texas in 1836. The North American settlers, who had been welcomed into that territory by the Mexican government itself, resisted the centralist program of the conservative government. After its victory at San Jacinto over the Mexican forces led by General Santa Ana, Texas proclaimed itself independent of Mexico. In the war against the United States, the admission of Texas to the Union in 1845 was the *casus belli*. Mexico was defeated and, under the Guadalupe Hidalgo Treaty of 1848, was obliged to renounce Texas and cede California and New Mexico to the United States for fifteen million dollars.

By 1850, Mexico still had not recovered the economic levels it had reached in the colonial period. The army continued to dominate public life and weighed heavily on the national economy. The government was continually defaulting and contracting new loans that went to swell its debts with international financiers; domestic creditors salvaged what they could from the situation.

STAGNATION AND ABSENCE OF POLITICAL HEGEMONY— PERU

The Peruvian mining economy, like the Mexican, was in total ruin, although it had already begun to decline by the end of the colonial period. To finance the wars, the royalists had intensified exploitation of the two mines still in operation, the Cerro del Pasco and Hualgayoc. When the Huancavelica quicksilver mine was shut down, the mercury needed for processing silver had to be imported, and San Martín himself offered Spain this monopoly. Later General Santa Cruz— then governing Bolivia—reopened the mine and offered to pay competitive prices to whoever would operate it. Labor was in short supply because men had been incorporated into the wars of the nineteenth century through conscription into the regular armies or into the *montoneros* (irregular troops). Furthermore, the mines "devoured" the men who were required to "enter the mines on Monday not to see the sun again until the following Sunday, never knowing whether it was day or night" (Viceroy Count de Lemos), a system that decimated the population.

Commerce was in as catastrophic a situation as mining. With the rupture of the link with Spain, the traditional trade routes dominated by Peru were eliminated. The alternative to the Isthmus of Panama was the more distant and dangerous Cape Horn, for which the Chilean port of Valparaiso was better situated. Guayaquil to the north and Valparaiso to the south became active rivals of El Callao. The agricultural output of the Peruvian sierra was isolated; the laws abolishing payment of tribute by the Indians and dividing the Indian lands changed nothing and failed to prevent these lands from gradually falling into private hands. As an immediate result, the city became increasingly divorced from the countryside, decentralization was encouraged, and systems of communication deteriorated. The agriculture of the coast, which had been based on irrigation and the use of slave labor, collapsed. Always closely tied to the commercial wealth of Lima, it was profoundly affected by the latter's decline. In these circumstances, the hacienda became even more autarchic both politically and economically. The army, which had been subordinate to civilian authority during the colonial period, now became the center of decision-making.

The history of Peru in those years continued to be bound up with that of Bolivia. A military man, Santa Cruz, who had seized power in Bolivia, created a confederation of Peru and Bolivia in 1836 and tried to carry out in Peru the administrative and judicial reforms that he had instituted in Bolivia. However, magistrates, functionaries, and merchants accustomed to tax evasion were alienated by his attempt to reorganize the fiscal system; the Lima aristocracy looked askance at a "protector" of such doubtful lineage; even the popular sectors were hostile because they were the first to suffer from the higher taxes; and the Indians felt themselves threatened by his policy of turning community lands into private property.

Santa Cruz also faced the opposition of neighboring Chile and Argentina. The former engaged Peru in war, largely to ensure the continued commercial hegemony of Valparaiso in the South Pacific. In its ranks fought some of Lima's disaffected "aristocracy." The Chilean victory put an end to the confederation, and Peru did not emerge from its stagnation until the mid-century boom in guano.

PROSPERITY AND STRUGGLES FOR HEGEMONY—
RIVER PLATE

The Independence wars and the rupture of the colonial pact had affected the economy and society of the old Viceroyalty of the River Plate at different levels. The economy needed to be reorganized and reinserted into the new conditions of the world market. This also involved regulating the labor of gauchos and estancia workers. The overriding problem of the period was the fixing of regional boundaries and the struggle for hegemony among the social groups. These different levels at which history unfolded were interrelated. If we devote more attention to the question of the supremacy of Buenos Aires among the United Provinces and the civil strife, this is because the political level was the channel and, to some extent, the expression of the other levels. Let us examine separately the various aspects of the formation of the national state in the River Plate.

The Independence wars began with the rebellion of the Cabildo of Buenos Aires—a local authority not directly appointed by the crown—against the Central Junta of Sevilla, which after the Napoleonic victories no longer enjoyed royal support. The fall of the Central Junta divested the Bourbon representatives in Spanish America of their last claim to legitimacy. Having gained control of Buenos Aires, the Independence forces made a double attempt at expansion, already revealing the national territorial ambitions of the Buenos Aires political group. Although Belgrano failed in his attempt to conquer Paraguay, an expedition penetrated Upper Peru, opening the way to the silver mines of Potosí, which had been the symbol and foundation of colonial wealth. These efforts to control not only the traditional trade route between Buenos Aires and the mines of Peru but also navigation on the Paraná River indicate the basic economic problems confronting the national states in the River Plate: the opening of routes and ports to assure exporting activities.

Later, in 1811, a counterattack mounted by the viceroy of Peru routed the Independence armies and closed the pass to Upper Peru. Thanks to Belgrano as well as to the pact made with Córdoba the previous year when advancing on Upper Peru, the retreating forces of Buenos Aires were able to secure alliances with local dominant groups in Tucumán and Salta. Nevertheless, defeat in Upper Peru shut off the trade of the River Plate with Puno on the edge of Lake Titicaca and with what is today Bolivia. On the other hand, control of traffic on the Upper Paraná River depended, from that time on, on the political evolution of Paraguay and on its alliances, whether with the province of Entre Ríos, the Banda Oriental (Uruguay), Buenos Aires, or Brazil.

The basin of the River Plate, or the Littoral, included Santa Fe and Corrientes on the same side as Buenos Aires, the Banda Oriental, or the east bank under the sway of Montevideo, on the opposite shore, and Entre Ríos in the middle. After Independence, Buenos Aires secured local support in the interior provinces of Córdoba, Tucumán, and Sala, as well as allies in Cuyo. At first the Littoral provinces also joined the new order, but this process was upset when the Banda Oriental came under the leadership of the Uruguayan caudillo Artigas, whose ideas of federalism and autonomy and whose democracy for the masses went against the establishment of a centralist national state controlled by Buenos Aires. The influence of Artigas as "Protector of the Free Peoples" spread beyond the Banda Oriental to Corrientes, Entre Ríos, Santa Fe, and even as far as Córdoba.

Although Buenos Aires supported the Uruguayans in their rebellion against the Spaniards, the Portuguese together with the English were interested in keeping Montevideo as an alternative port to Buenos Aires, and wanted an armistice between the Artigas forces and centralist troops commanded by Buenos Aires. After 1814, when a Buenos Aires expedition under General Alvear forced the capitulation of troops loyal to Spain in Montevideo, the victorious invaders fought against Artigas and his democratizing influence. For this reason, Artigas was compelled to accept Portuguese intervention and the annexation of the Banda Oriental to the Portuguese Empire under the name of the Cisplatine Province in 1816.

To consolidate a centralist republic under its hegemony, Buenos Aires convened in 1813 a constituent assembly, which created the United Provinces of the River Plate. In 1816 it convened a congress in Tucumán. Obstacles were raised by the federalism of several provinces and by the local economic interests, which saw in the centralism of Buenos Aires a threat to their fiscal and economic independence.

Buenos Aires was in fact governed politically by a military group organized in the Lautaro Lodge, a secret association modeled after the Masonic lodge. It was also involved in the struggle for independence on the other side of the Andes where San Martín, allied with O'Higgins, was trying to liberate Chile. Inspired by the French Revolution and headed by Pueyrredón, the Buenos Aires directorate sought to impose a centralist constitution and perhaps even establish a monarchy. This shattered the unity of the provinces.

After the disintegration of the centralist constitution in 1820, Artigas-style federalism (even though its founder had fled from the Portuguese to exile in Paraguay) and local economic interests again arrested the centralism of Buenos Aires. Both the provincial autonomists and their concrete social expression, *caudillismo,* recovered their importance. Between 1819 and 1825 many provinces drew up their own constitutions. Santiago del Estero separated from Tucumán at the beginning of 1820, followed by Catamarca in 1821; Salta and Jujuy broke away from the central power, and the province of Mendoza lost control of San Juan; Córdoba and Corrientes proclaimed their constitutions in 1821, and Entre Ríos in 1822.

The movement was based economically on cattle raising, mule trade with Upper Peru, and local craft industries. The country estancia and the provincial caudillo with his armed guard opposed the Illustrious United Republic. The latter, thanks chiefly to the influence of Rivadavia, enjoyed a parliamentary and secularized government without equal in the history of the United Provinces. The province of Buenos Aires had been untouched by the wars and rebellions that disrupted the economic base of the other provinces. Furthermore, although its leaders had been staunch defenders of unity up until 1820, the province of Buenos Aires benefited from the new federalist spirit because it did not have to support the cost of a national organization to maintain wartime armies.

Meanwhile, Buenos Aires underwent significant economic and social changes.[2] The foundation of the colonial wealth of Buenos Aires was deeply affected by the elimination of the colonial trade monopolies after 1810 and by the interruption of the traditional route between Buenos Aires and the Pacific by way of the mines of Upper Peru. The Independence forces of Buenos Aires had failed to gain mastery of this route, and it subsequently lost importance when Europe began to trade directly with the ports of the Pacific.

Colonial wealth had been concentrated in the import-export trade, in urban properties, and in the hands of agents of the metropolitan companies. After Independence, inflation made investment in real estate unprofitable and reduced the value of colonial mercantile capital. Commercial investment also suffered from the activities of British merchants based in Liverpool. Local business was slow to adapt to the new movement of commerce and, moreover, was dominated by the British. The *porteño* capitalists ultimately found that the best way to adapt themselves to the changed economic conditions was to return to the countryside, especially after 1820. Thus, the development of cattle raising in Buenos Aires province was financed with the commercial capital accumu-

2. See Tulio Halperín Donghi, "La expansión ganadera en la campaña de Buenos Aires," *Desarrollo Económico* (Buenos Aires), vol. 3, no. 122, especially pp. 71–72. The analysis that follows is based on this work.

lated during the colonial period. Foreign merchants, principally English, also participated in this process. Once the flow of Peruvian silver ended, and once it became necessary to export in order to pay for imports from Great Britain, the exports of hides had to solve the balance-of-payments problems. British merchants also operated the River Plate meat-salting plants on the southern edge of the continent. The meat-salting industry sustained the growth of Buenos Aires by supplementing the market for hides—which fluctuated in price according to exports from Russia and not according to demand—with a new group of consumers.

As silver grew scarce and became subject to speculation, its export was prohibited. Merchants and cattle ranchers were the intermediaries in these negotiations. They accepted the substitution of paper currency for coins, thereby benefiting from later revaluations; they furnished bills of exchange to permit Buenos Aires to carry on business with foreign markets; and they still managed to transfer silver abroad despite the prohibition.

The prosperity produced by trade in hides changed *porteño* society. The merchants turned *estancieros* became prominent in local society. Even the owners of meat-salting plants —like Juan Manuel de Rosas and Dorrego, who both played important roles in the political consolidation of Buenos Aires —were of urban-commercial origin and only recently linked to agriculture. It was "a group lacking a strong rural tradition but closely tied to the political class of urban origin and to the new elements that dominated porteño commercial life."[3]

The estancia, basis of export agriculture, needed labor and land in order to expand. Both these requirements depended on the military organization. The Independence wars between provinces had depleted the regular army, so groups of estancieros armed their own rural militias. With this military power, they set about to extend the frontiers of Buenos

3. *Ibid.*, p. 87.

Aires Province. It was the estancieros—not only those dating from the colonial period but also the new and foreign ones—who gave impulse to the expansion that was to serve as a basis for reconciliation of the conflicts among owners of meat-salting plants, local merchants, and the political oligarchy of the city.

Rosas symbolized this new period, on both an economic and a political level, as plunderer of Indian lands and owner of the largest meat-salting plant in Buenos Aires. Nevertheless, the 1820s were still influenced by the centralist elite of Buenos Aires. The Cisplatine Province, which had won its independence under the command of Lavalleja, abandoned the federalist policy of Artigas to support Buenos Aires centralism in the Congress of Florida (1825). This influenced the delegates to accept a centralized national organization. The constitution of 1826 created the Argentine Republic, and Rivadavia was elected its president. Centralism appeared finally to have obtained a consensus.

Nevertheless, landholders and merchants, as well as the ecclesiastic and conservative groups that distrusted Rivadavia's liberalism in domestic matters, now regarded centralism with suspicion. In 1827, the provinces, including Buenos Aires, rejected the national constitution, and the union remained together only because its support of the Uruguayans had involved it in a war against Brazil.

Behind the insurrection against Brazil of the Banda Oriental—as Uruguay was called—existed a change in English policy. The new English government, with Canning as its foreign minister, backed the Argentine liberal commercial groups against the colonial groups that favored first the Portuguese and then the Brazilians. The aim of Canning's policy was to secure the autonomy of Montevideo as an alternative to the port of Buenos Aires, in order to control at least one port in two different countries for British trade.

Although Argentina won the battle of Paso de Rosario (Ituzaingó) in the war against Brazilians, Rivadavia sent an emissary to Brazil who signed an agreement to respect Brazil's dominion over the Cisplatine Province. The reason for the agreement was that Buenos Aires had alone borne almost all the costs of the war and was suffering the economic consequences of its action. Rivadavia was compelled to disavow his representative and subsequently he even had to resign.

After the fall of Rivadavia, General Dorrego succeeded to the presidency. Under pressure from the English, he signed a peace treaty with Brazil that guaranteed the independence of the Cisplatine Province, then baptized the Oriental Republic of Uruguay. When the Argentine army returned from Uruguay, it deposed and executed Dorrego. The military commanders of the war against Brazil were Generals Lavalle and Paz. Lavalle controlled Buenos Aires. Paz, after defeating the caudillos Bustos of Cordoba and Facundo Quiroga of La Rioja, asserted his authority over nine provinces of the interior. Both were centralists, and their deposing of Dorrego was a victory over federalism. The victory was short-lived.

Juan Manuel de Rosas, leader of the Buenos Aires federalists, united with the caudillo López of Santa Fe against this new centralist position. In 1829 his forces of rural militia and federalist caudillos defeated Lavalle and he declared himself governor of the Province of Buenos Aires. From then on and after the capture of General Paz, the supremacy of Rosas and with him of Buenos Aires was undisputed. An agreement called the Littoral Pact was concluded between the river-basin provinces of Corrientes and Buenos Aires, Entre Ríos and Santa Fe.

Rosas held power in Buenos Aires from 1831 to 1852. These were also the years of expansion of livestock production and consolidation of the estancieros of the "humid pampa." The social base of his rule was the exploitation of farm labor and the incorporation of the rural marginal population into the labor force or the army. The legal instrument of repression used by the estancieros was the formation of rural militias and the placing of their sympathizers in the judicial and police apparatus in order to guarantee labor discipline on the estancia. Halperin sums up the functioning of this system and its favorable effects on expansion of livestock production:

> By forcing the marginal population into groups of wage
> labor and by effectively curbing the illegal activities
> through which local merchants had kept their indepen-
> dence and contested the supremacy of the hacendados,
> the police and judicial organization that had been estab-
> lished in the countryside immediately after 1820 and
> consolidated during the regime of Rosas gave decisive
> aid to the hegemony of the hacendados.[4]

Together with this system of repression, the perpetual indebtedness of the farm workers and the "modernization"—
that is, the rationalization and intensification of labor, especially in the south of Buenos Aires Province—ensured the
success of the cattle-ranch economy. It should be pointed out,
however, that during this period the incorporation of the
River Plate economy into the export system was accomplished
without the abundant labor that had been available in the
colonial period, and this acted not only as a corrective to
police repression but also as a spur to more efficient use of
labor in the southern part of the country.

The economic success of the Rosas Regime served to
strengthen the position of Buenos Aires in Argentina's foreign policy. Newly converted to federalism, which under the
circumstances meant the economic domination of Buenos
Aires Province and its port, the elite groups in Buenos Aires
fought the centralists of the interior. They also maintained
their interest in control of navigation on the Paraná and Uruguay rivers and, consequently, in the policy of the Banda
Oriental.

Foreign powers sought to keep river traffic and trade
with the interior open. This brought them into conflict with
Buenos Aires. In Uruguay, English and Brazilian interests
supported the Colorado party and its head, Fructuoso Rivera,
even though he had been a leader of the insurgents of the Rio

4. *Ibid.*, p. 97.

Grande del Sur against the Brazilian Empire. The Rosas policy was also under pressure from the French who—like the English but with less of a Latin America tradition and less experience in imperialism—tried to keep open river traffic and trade in the Littoral by securing allies among the centralists. After overcoming a French blockade in 1840, Rosas adopted a bolder policy with Uruguay thanks to the defection of Oribe. The latter, having been elected president by Rivera's Colorado party and then compelled to resign in October 1838 by his former protector, went over to Rosas and became a general in the army of the United Provinces.

This episode further demonstrated the lack of national identity in the River Plate region until the middle of the nineteenth century. All subsequent policy would be aimed at gaining control of Buenos Aires—on the one hand, by the Brazilians, and on the other, by the English and French, who wanted to keep Montevideo as an alternative to the port of Buenos Aires as well as in the interior provinces, in order to expand their trade.

After Oribe joined forces with Rosas, there was constant strife in Uruguay. The country was divided, with some regions under the Colorados and others under the opposition Blancos. In an attempt to intervene in the River Plate, Brazil sought support locally and in Europe. It even sent a mission to England and France to negotiate an armed invasion, which the Brazilian foreign minister stipulated was to guarantee the independence of Uruguay. In the face of irreconcilable differences with the French and English views, Brazil withdrew its proposal. Increased pressure by European diplomacy, especially by France, in the second half of the 1840s resulted in a blockade of Montevideo and control of the rivers.

Meanwhile, the position of Rosas had been strengthened by the economic prosperity of Buenos Aires. His attitude toward Brazil was sometimes one of conciliation but more often one of distrust. In 1843 a treaty was signed with the Empire, which Rosas later rejected because the Brazilians supported the Colorados and did not recognize Oribe as president after his resignation.

The policy of Rosas broke down when members of the United Provinces turned against him. In 1847, the monopolistic interests of the porteño bourgeoisie closed the port of Rosario, which was used by the exporters of Entre Ríos. Urquiza, general and caudillo of Entre Ríos, found allies in the province of Corrientes, in the Uruguayans opposed to Oribe, and in the Brazilians. Oribe was captured in 1851, and Rosas, after the battle of Monte Caseros where he was defeated by the new alliance, went into exile in Europe. With the support of the old centralists and the new victors, an Argentine confederation once more became viable. In 1853, the federal constitution, influenced by the long-time liberal Alberdi, provided for a strong central government. Under this constitution, General Urquiza was elected the first president, and his authoritarian rule brought about political unity, continued economic expansion, and—most important for foreign interests—internationalized navigation on the Paraná and Uruguay Rivers. Uruguay also benefited from these developments. Its neutrality and free access to river traffic and trade were, in those years, the basic conditions for the national liberty of Uruguay.

"BOURGEOIS OLIGARCHY" AND "OLIGARCHIC BOURGEOISIE"—CHILE

In the first half of the nineteenth century, the Chilean situation seemed exceptional among Spanish-American countries. By 1833, Chile already had reasonably stable political institutions. In the reorganization of Latin American relations with the metropolitan market, the Chilean port Valparaiso was well situated. In addition to the precious metals, Chile's numerous exports included copper, for which there were favorable prospects on the world market. Its agricultural and livestock exports had good prospects as well.

The period of "anarchy" was short, but there were seven years of strife among the military caudillos, who dragged the upper classes of Chilean society into their conflicts. Some historians contend that the "aristocratic frond" incited the caudillos against each other and that "basically, the frond was after power for itself."[5] This would have required the upper classes to suppress their old rivalries and reconcile their interests. The minister-dictator Diego Portales attempted just this. Edward Vives says:

> The work of Portales was the restoration of a fact and a sentiment that had served as the basis for public order during the Octavian peace of the three centuries of colonial rule—the fact was a strong and durable power, superior to the prestige of a caudillo and to the force of a faction; the sentiment was the traditional respect for abstract authority, for power independently exercised by the legitimately established regime. He made a new idea out of an old one."[6]

Aníbal Pinto remarks:

> The political creation of Portales was the institution of colonial forms under a republican structure. . . . It may be exactly the opposite case—that Portales established or drafted republican forms for the socio-economic structure of the old regime, which essentially did not change one iota in its passage to the status of Independence.[7]

A glance at the functioning of the economy may give us a clue to where the truth really lies. The author just quoted refers to the spectacular rise of the export sector. Exports between 1844 and 1860 quadrupled in value, and

5. Albert Edwards Vives, *La fronda aristocrática* (Santiago: Ercilla, 1936), p. 36.

6. *Ibid.*, p. 39.

7. Aníbal Pinto, *Chile, un caso de desarrollo frustrado* (Santiago: Editorial Universitaria, 1959), p. 15.

this was a rate of increase that was already under way. In mining, the boom in silver was reached with the opening of the Chanarcillo mine in 1832; copper later came to represent at its peak 40 percent of world production, and it supplied 65 percent of the needs of British industry and consumption. Agriculture continued to be important in exports. Even before Independence, shipments of wheat to the traditional Peruvian market amounted to more than 145,000 quintales (hundredweight). Agricultural production in 1844–1860 went up five times, and its proportion in the export total in 1844–1880 (although not the period under discussion, it furnishes an idea) reached an average of 45 percent.

Tulio Halperin perhaps came closest to finding the key to the Chilean experience in the alliance between the traditional landholding class closely bound to the export sector and the newer mining wealth no less interested in preserving the established order.[8] With Chile's victory over the Confederation of Peru and Bolivia in 1839, the power of these classes was consolidated and fully expressed in the commercial hegemony of Valparaiso.

Consolidation of External Linkage and the Bourgeois-Oligarchic Domination

In the years following 1850, almost all the Latin American countries entered a period of greater prosperity. The economic order at the international level was better integrated around the metropolitan powers. Trade, which until that time had been relatively small in volume, began to grow. The gold rush in California and a little later in Australia not only increased trade but also gave rise to waves of migration that affected the American countries. This was the period dealt with by Vicente Pérez Rosales in his delightful description of the adventures of Chileans in California. California

---

8. Halperín Donghi, *Historia contemporánea*, p. 205.

and Australia opened up economic space, even if they were controlled by the metropolitan powers.

Expansion and better integration into the world market was made possible by new means of transport, especially maritime. The steamboat, which had been tried out in the 1820s on the Magdalena and Plate rivers, was in general use by the 1840s for both river navigation and the Pacific coastal traffic of Peru and Chile. This was nonetheless accompanied by a significant increase in the use of traditional New England clipper ships on the Cape Horn route.

The importation of consumer goods, principally textiles, on which Latin America had depended until 1850 and which often has adverse effects on the balance of payments, became less important. Extension of railway transport required the importation of capital goods like iron and steel, coal, and replacement parts. The new market stimulated Latin America to develop an industrial economy—Chilean copper was an excellent example—and there was a rising demand for food-stuffs in the metropolitan areas. Better integration and increased demand led many countries to specialize in one export product. Accompanying these developments was an expansion of the financial sector. Banks were established in the principal cities. By channeling foreign credit and the flow of new capital, they began to orient investment and business. Most of these banking and financial institutes depended on or were closely linked to the City of London.

Although the period favored expansion, Latin America also suffered the repercussions of a series of world economic crises in 1857, 1866, 1873, 1882, and later those of 1890 and 1900. Actually, until 1890 these crises depressed the prices of industrial goods more than those of raw materials. Nevertheless, the Latin American economy was continually in debt to foreign creditors, and these debts had to be paid in specie. Inflation and the domestic issue of nonconvertible bank notes were resorted to, with the burden falling on the weakest sectors of society. On the other hand, the frequent crises were rapidly overcome and the system continued to function.

The transformation of Latin America's external linkage was closely related to the structure of its internal economy, especially to the expansion of private land holdings. The second half of the nineteenth century began almost everywhere with the appropriation of Indian lands often accompanied by the appropriation of Church properties. In some countries this process was accelerated by export possibilities: the increase of production required more land. In others it was due to the enterprise of domestic groups that foresaw the rising demand in local cities and towns. Participating in the emerging expansion of the economy were the traditional local merchants who had been displaced by the British, and in the case of Argentina, groups that until then had not figured in the ruling classes, as well as the ruling classes themselves.

Mexico provided a good example of land appropriation.[9] On June 25, 1856, the "Ley Lerdo" was promulgated and contained the following provisions:

1. Religious and civil corporations were prohibited from owning any property not essential to the carrying out of their activities.

2. Church properties were to be transferred to their tenants at a value to be estimated by capitalizing annual rental income at six percent.

3. In case the tenants refused to purchase the property, the latter would be subject to "denunciation," with the "denouncer" receiving one-eighth of the value of said property.

4. The Church might use the product from the sale of its rural and urban holdings to buy shares in industrial and agricultural enterprises.

One consequence, perhaps unforeseen, was that the law was applied equally to the Indian communities. Furthermore, although the law was designed to benefit the tenants, these were almost always too ignorant and poor to take advantage of its provisions. Therefore, the "denouncers" were either

9. See Jesús Silva Herzog, *Breve historia de la revolución mexicana* (Mexico: Fondo de Cultura Economica, 1960).

wealthy merchants or large landholders who extended their property by incorporating mortmain. The process was irreversible. After overthrowing the Liberal authors of the Reform, the Conservatives, who had joined the French intervention with Maximilian in 1864, continued the policy of land appropriation, thanks to which many high-ranking officers of the French army became hacendados.

In Guatemala, the liberal revolution only came in 1871. The process was tied to the expansion of coffee as an export product.[10] Huge tracts of uncultivated or public lands were taken over, and when no more Church lands were available, the communal lands of the Indians were appropriated. Although these lands were not entirely incorporated into a market system, they had to be tilled. Members of the former Indian communities were forced into a subsistence economy, to be used as additional labor force by landlords only when needed.

Many labor practices in agriculture date from this period, when the peasant was given the use of a small piece of land where he could grow his food crops and in exchange was obliged to perform the labor required of him by the landlord. This system of labor also predominated in the Andes of South America. As in Mexico, Guatemala, and other countries, the peasant was kept in perpetual debt to the landlord so that he was never actually paid wages. Wage-earning peasants were thought to be "not only too expensive but also too independent." The hacendado had the right to limit the size of the peasant's plot of land and to oblige him to consume a fixed quantity of staples, a method of indebtedness guaranteed to discipline labor. Even more drastic ways of obtaining labor were used in Guatemala and elsewhere; colonial laws were revived and *habilitaciones*, or forced-labor gangs, were used on the coffee plantations. The "habilitaciones" permitted

10. See Edelberto Torres Rivas, *Procesos y estructuras de una sociedad dependiente: Centroamérica* (Santiago: Ediciones Prensa Latinoamericana, 1969).

local authorities to compel Indians to work for minimal wages or for nothing, using such pretexts as payment of nonexistent debts and payment of fines.[11]

Labor supply was a permanent problem. With the disappearance of the slave traffic, immigration was promoted as another solution. Chinese coolies were introduced chiefly into Cuba, Peru, Mexico, and Panama.[12] As was already mentioned, the plantation economy of coastal Peru depended on slave labor, and when in 1854 General Castilla abolished slavery and the Indian head-tax, the labor situation worsened. Ships were sent to Chinese ports, where they collected workers who were then landed in Peru to be "sold" to domestic employers on eight-year enforceable work contracts. The contract obliged the employer to dress, house, and pay the worker wages of one sol (silver coin then worth one dollar) weekly. The price of a Chinese coolie varied from three hundred to four hundred soles. It is estimated that 74,952 coolies entered Peru between 1860 and 1874 and that 7,677 died in transit.

In Cuba, the labor shortage reached crisis proportions by the middle of the century. The first expedient readily at hand was the use of Mexican Indians from Yucatan, who, with the complicity of the local authorities, were forcibly brought in as "contract workers." A little later Chinese coolies were used. In August 1878, the *Revista Económica* of Havana published figures showing that about 125,000 Chinese had entered Cuba between 1853 and 1874 and that their price ranged from one hundred to four hundred dollars per coolie.

In Brazil similar measures were taken to cope with the scarcity of labor. Around 1844, a powerful coffee plantation owner, Senator Vergueiro, contracted workers directly in Europe. Having persuaded the government to finance their travel, he settled eighty German families on his São Paulo

11. *Ibid.*
12. See Gustavo Beyhaut, *America centrale e meridionale: dall'indipendenza alla crisi attuale* (Milan: Feltrinelli Editore, 1968), translated from Spanish by Laura Ingrao.

plantation. After 1852 others followed suit, bringing in *colonos* who were mainly Italian, Spanish, and Portuguese.

The Latin American countries were linked to the international market through a variety of products: the wheat and copper of Chile; the wool and livestock of the River Plate; the guano of Peru; the coffee of Venezuela, Brazil, Colombia, and Central America; and the sugar of the West Indies, Brazil, Mexico, and Peru. It is interesting to note that these products could still be developed with national capital and that there were sufficient local resources to finance diversified and large-scale undertakings. In his book Aníbal Pinto cites:

> Neither his fortune nor his advanced age could dull the enterprising spirit of Urmeneta. He established the Guayacán and Tongoy foundries and brought from Europe the most skillful chemists and administrators. He opened two ports in the north, developed a coal field in the south, and purchased a fleet of steamers in Europe. Based in Santiago, he was the promoter of almost all the advances made by Chile in the second third of the nineteenth century. He headed the Southern Railway, introduced gas lighting, and invested large sums of money in industries that failed: the manufacture of beet sugar, silk, fine cloth, and coarse wool textiles. In his hacienda of Limace he cultivated vineyards and orchards and planted the first eucalyptus trees.[13]

Most foreign investment entered markerting and interoceanic transport, whereas local investment continued to be limited to the primary activities, which meant that production was controlled nationally while marketing and transportation were controlled from abroad. This pattern changed later with the flow of foreign investment mainly into the extractive industries. What was the reason for this division of functions between locals and foreigners? Corruption and bribery certainly played a role, but the explanation given by

13. Francisco Encina, *Historia de Chile,* quoted by Aníbal Pinto, *op. cit.*, p. 18.

Halperín seems to correspond more nearly to the facts. Foreign investment in these sectors increased the income of the local landowner by expanding production. Furthermore, as the value of his land rose, so did the landowner's capital, without his having had to make any significant outlay. It was not a question of whether local capital was available for the investments made by foreigners; the fact was that the owners of this capital, when they existed, were not interested in investing it in such activities.

Expansion of the railway grid, nonetheless, required a volume of investment beyond the possibilities of local private capital, although the latter participated in some cases. Foreign investment was substantial but not total, and the role of public investment was preponderant. Railroad development was different in each country. In Argentina, Chile, Mexico, and Uruguay, national railway systems were created; in Brazil and Peru, production centers were connected with ports by foreign-owned railways, although in the former country interior railways were under national control.

Foreign lending, now facilitated by the greater volume of capital available in the metropolitan powers, entered the political scene. Governments could become more independent of the rural sectors that had been the traditional source of fiscal revenue; the state was consolidated as an institution.

External linkage was further reinforced by a free trade policy which from 1850 on was increasingly practiced by all the countries. Several factors encouraged this policy; the important groups were producers of primary products or engaged in related services.

> All were more or less free traders for the same reason; their principal markets were abroad and so was the source of the commodities they required to satisfy their generally refined tastes. They were not protectionists for the simple reason that they had little to protect.[14]

14. Aníbal Pinto, *op. cit.*, p. 39.

Growing urbanization increased the number of people that depended on imported articles.

Loss of Control of the Export Sector by the National Bourgeoisie

Although some countries were able to maintain the division of functions outlined above, others could not keep foreign interests—chiefly from the United States or Great Britain—from gaining control of national production sectors.

Various primary activities, especially mining, began to require large capital investment as well as increasingly complex transportation and marketing services. The position of the economies that had to face strong imperialist competition was weakened by their growing financial and commercial dependence; and the position of the landholding classes was also undermined in various ways, despite their political, commercial, and financial ties. Some examples of the loss of economic control by national producers can be given, beginning with those linked to the English and European powers.

ALIENATION OF THE NITRATE INDUSTRY—CHILE

The Peruvian government exercised a monopoly over its nitrate deposits, having compensated the former owners with bonds issued by the state. After Peru's defeat in the War of the Pacific, its nitrate deposits were taken over by Chile, which did not assume any obligation for redemption of the bonds. The debt continued to be Peruvian, and the bonds ceased to be quoted on the financial market.

Some time later the bonds were purchased by "mysterious buyers"—some Englishmen—for 10 to 20 percent of their nominal value and in depreciated soles. In 1881, the Chilean government decided to return the nitrate deposits to the certificate holders, who then became the owners of the major part of the industry. A central figure in this drama—as absurd as it was disreputable—was the almost legendary John T. North, who ironically enough used Chilean capital provided by the Bank of Valparaiso for the speculation that turned him into the "nitrate king." North and his associates received from this institution and "other" Chilean moneylenders six million pesos to buy up the nitrate certificates and the Tarapacá railway. Demoralization quickly set in and extended, curiously enough, to the point of reducing the part of the industry that had been controlled by the Chileans before the conflict.

In 1878, British–North American capital represented 13 percent and Peruvian-Chilean capital 67 percent of the industry: the remaining 20 percent belonged to foreigners whose assets had been nationalized. By August 1, 1884, Peruvian capital had disappeared; Chilean capital was reduced to 36 percent; British capital reached 34 percent; and nonnationalized European capital 30 percent. On December 31, 1901, British capital accounted for 55 percent; nationalized European capital, 30 percent; and Chilean capital, 15 percent.[15] Another scholar has shown how the nitrate interests were linked to Chilean political groups, the most common procedure being to name party officials and congressmen as lawyers or representatives for the companies.[16]

GUANO AND THE DREYFUS COMPANY—PERU[17]

It was Piérola as minister of finance who conceived the project that resulted in turning guano exploitation over to foreign firms. The basis of his policy was that the profits remaining in the country could be distributed through the state apparatus to economic groups with political influence. National capitalists who previously had enjoyed state concessions to run the industry (even though the transportation system and commercialization were controlled by foreign enterprises)

15. Francisco Encina, *Historia de Chile,* quoted by Aníbal Pinto, *op. cit.,* p. 55.

16. See Hernán Ramírez Necochea, *Balmaceda y la contrarevolución de 1891* (Santiago: Editorial Universitaria, 1958).

17. See E. Yepes del Castillo, *Peru 1820-1920: un siglo de desarrollo capitalista* (Lima: Instituto de Estudios Peruanos, Campodónico Ediciones, 1972).

opposed the scheme, and they were supported by the supreme court, the permanent commission, and most of the press. Piérola was anxious to favor the Dreyfus Company—which had itself enlisted local support—and after removing five recalcitrant ministers, he finally decided to carry the matter to a rubber-stamp congress. He based his proposal on the construction of a railway that would be financed by the sale of guano. Because everyone was infected with the railway fever and expected a wave of prosperity from public works, it was a question not of taking sides with either the Dreyfus Company or the concessionaires but of waiting for the shower of gold that Peru would receive from the sale of two million tons of guano.[18]

THE UNITED PRESENCE

In 1902 Venezuela was involved in a conflict with its European creditors that led to joint coercion by Great Britain, Germany, and Italy. At this point, the United States, which had already intervened in Mexico, established its presence in Latin America by proclaiming the Roosevelt Corollary to the Monroe Doctrine. The United States declared that if a Latin American state became chronically remiss in payment of contracted debts, only the United States could compel that state to make the reforms necessary to reach a settlement, even though this would benefit European and not United States creditors. In subsequent years, the United States did not hesitate to apply the new corollary of its doctrine.

Initially, the weight of United States intervention was felt most heavily in the Caribbean and Central American areas. The latter acquired great strategic significance in the second half of the nineteenth century because it was crossed by one of the most important lines of communication between the Atlantic and Pacific coasts of North America. Political

18. Pedro Dávalos y Sissen, *La primera centura,* quoted by E. Yepes, *ibid.*

expansion also figured prominently in the Caribbean and Central American areas: the second Independence War of Cuba in 1896 led to the Spanish-American War of 1898; the Treaty of Paris made the United States master of Puerto Rico and the dominant power in Cuba. There were further interventions: Panama in 1917, 1918, and 1925; Haiti, occupied by the marines from 1915 to 1934; the Dominican Republic, occupied from 1916 to 1924; Nicaragua, occupied by the marines from 1912 to 1925; and in Mexico, the disembarcation in Veracruz of 1914 and the Pershing Expedition of 1916.

The case of Panama Canal is illustrative. After the de Lesseps project had failed, its creditors set up a New Company to sell its concession to the United States, which had showed some interest in taking over the project. In 1903, Colombia signed a treaty confirming the rights previously acquired by the New Company by which the country constructing the canal would be ceded a strip of land ten miles wide from ocean to ocean. The Colombian senate refused to ratify the treaty, and on November 3 a revolution led by local agents of the New Company proclaimed the independence of the Republic of Panama. On November 6, the United States recognized the new Republic, and on November 18 Secretary of State Hay signed an agreement with Bunau-Varilla, who had been the chief engineer of the New Company and now represented Panama in Washington. This treaty contained essentially the provisions that had been rejected by the Colombian senate; in exchange for sovereign rights in perpetuity over the ten-mile-wide Canal Zone stretching from the capital of Panama to its principal port on the Atlantic, the United States granted Panama an annual subsidy and guaranteed its independence—a function which it had already begun to perform during the Panamanian revolution when its gunboats had stood by to prevent the landing of Colombian troops.

After World War I, the United States presence, which had been concentrated in the area under discussion, expanded rapidly into South America. The countries of the Pacific were totally incorporated into its economy, and in the Atlantic, Brazil and even Uruguay and Argentina came under its influence.

United States expansion had new and interesting features. Its investments seemed to be less closely linked than the British to the consumption needs of the metropolitan power and directed more to local markets. This did not diminish the importance of its investments in industries tied to the United States market, such as mining and plantations of tropical fruits. The monopolistic and oligopolistic character of the large United States enterprises began to dominate production. Often the budget of one of these enterprises would be many times greater than that of many Latin American states. Moreover, United States foreign policy supported the interests of the United States firms. A final example will give an idea of the process:

> The banana, which had begun to assume importance as an export commodity, was cultivated locally and transported in foreign merchant ships to the Atlantic coast of the United States. In 1901 the Guatemalan government, representing local plantation owners, signed an agreement with the United Fruit Company for regular transportation of its banana output. On August 31 of the previous year it had contracted with the "Central Improvement Company" to terminate a railway connecting the Atlantic and Pacific oceans in order to facilitate overland transportation of national production. The first liberal government had begun construction of the railway in 1874, completing 136 miles. For the 61 remaining miles, Guatemala ceded to the Company control of the railway for 99 years, the dock facilities of Puerto Barrios, a strip of land for installations on either side of the railway, tax exemption, and free importation of materials. The firm finished building the railway in 1908. Through a series of complicated negotiations, the transport company, on the one hand, began to produce and market its own output, thereby displacing local planters to the

north; on the other hand, when the International Railways of Central America (a subsidiary of the United Fruit Company) took over the entire national railway system, the United Fruit Company completed the process of monopolization of banana production and national transport.[19]

National Control of the Production System

The control of the production system by local enterprises after Independence was neither uniform in the history of the Latin American countries nor without obstacles. Declarations of independence in each country were followed by bitter struggles among the various local groups. From these struggles—known as the "anarchic" period of national histories—emerged the alliances mentioned earlier, national markets, and the territorial limits set by the dominant groups to affirm the legitimacy or effectiveness of the order they had established. In an initial situation of underdevelopment and dependence, the groups that "forged independence" renewed their links with the world market and with other local groups. This situation could be characterized as follows:

The world capitalist system, dominated by Great Britain, was related to the periphery through its need for raw materials. British industrial expansion depended, not necessarily on investment of production capital in the periphery, but on assuring its own supply of primary products. For that reason, European investments were directed mainly toward the sectors that local economies were not competent to develop; for example, transport. Even this sector did not receive direct investment, but received loans, guaranteed by the state, to finance local works. Although the dominant center actually controlled the marketing of the output of the periphery, it did not replace the local economic class that inherited its production base from the colony. The only important exception

19. E. Torres, *op. cit.*, pp. 45–46.

was mining, and even in this case local owners coexisted with foreign investors.

Because the new hegemonic center did not hinder and, in some cases, even stimulated expansion of local production, the end of the colonial pact strengthened national producing groups when the latter could organize a system of alliances with "local oligarchies" to consolidate a national state. This undertaking was conditioned as much by the "market situation" directed by the group that controlled port facilities, the basic production sector, and so forth, as by the capacity of some segments of the dominant class to establish a political system of control. A national administration and a national— not a regional or a personal—army were crucial in building a state apparatus and transforming de facto power into de jure government; these processes were carried out at different periods and with varying degrees of similarity by Portales in Chile, Rosas in Argentina, and the Regency in Brazil, to cite only a few examples.

From an economic point of view, the success of the national economies in this situation depended on (1) availability of a primary product to ensure, transform, and develop the export sector inherited from the colony; (2) an abundant labor supply; and (3) availability of lands for distribution as private property. The last two production factors were essential for direct capital formation, since they permitted entrepreneurs to accumulate capital irrespective of "savings decisions." That is to say, to accumulate capital, under the above listed circumstances, it was enough to appropriate land directly through occupation without payment and to exploit a cheap labor force. The low degree of equipment required for that type of labor-intensive economy implied a very small level of direct investment of money in the productive system.

In these circumstances, it is easy to understand that, at the local level, expansion of the export economy was more a political than an economic problem. To ensure the availability of land and labor, local dominant groups had to ally themselves with landowners who were marginal to the export system. Not only was the otherwise weak political administration of the export group reinforced by these landowners who kept order in their unproductive latifundia, but the labor supply was maintained by the exclusion of peasant farmers, immigrants, and liberated slaves from owning property.

The foregoing reveals the relation between the "modern" group, composed of the export-economy sectors, and the "traditional" group. Although the former established a national system to favor its own interests, it also allied itself with the latter to safeguard those same interests. Nevertheless, differences between the two groups did not disappear with this alliance; local oligarchies often fought exporting groups for a larger share in income distribution.[20]

The exporting groups, plantation and mine owners, merchants and bankers, played a vital intermediary role between European and American economies and the "traditional" agricultural sectors. National political institutions had to serve not only the interests of the "modernizing" groups created by the export system itself but also the interests of the regional oligarchies, which usually opposed any effort to convert the dominant paternalism into a more efficient bureaucracy. Political contradictions between the dominant sectors continued into the twentieth century when, with the success of the export model of integration into the world economy, new groups like the urban-industrial, the urban-commercial, and the service sector were added to the national economy of some countries. Subsequently, the middle class began to make political reforms that reconciled the divergent interests of the dominant groups.[21]

Peripheral nations control their own production in two ways: (1) since, to cope with world market demands, "national policies" concerning export products are required, investment is subject to internal decision on whether to expand

20. This was the case in the Farrapos war, when the livestock producers of jerked beef in southern Brazil fought against the Empire, as also occurred in the battles between the provinces and Buenos Aires.

21. These divergencies tended to diminish when the "popular

or reduce output; (2) this means that the process of capital accumulation is internal in a specific way: land and labor force are controlled by local entrepreneurs, and national political decisions that reinforce bourgeois control over productive systems are indirectly determined by the entrepreneurs, through its control over the state apparatus.

Nevertheless, marketing of exports depends on prices, quotas, and so forth imposed in the international market by those who control it in the central economies.

Chances of Latin American countries to integrate into the world market as dependent but developing economies are closely related to the ability of local producers to reorient their political and economic links both internally and externally. Externally, the terms of negotiation are set by the financial and commercial sectors of the central economies and their local agents, which means that the marketing apparatus of the local economies must be reoriented in order to eliminate "colonial interests" and benefit the new dynamic centers of capitalism, thereby modifying international political alliances. Internally, "national order" is established and a state is created through struggles and alliances with the oligarchies relegated to a secondary position in the export sector or excluded from it. Thus, an alliance is formed between what is known in sociology as the modern "plantation" with its urban commercial and financial groups and the traditional "hacienda." From the end of the period of "anarchy" (1850) to the crisis of the outward-growth model (1930), these two basic forms were the pillars of Latin American society and political organization in the countries whose economies do not belong to enclave type of linkage to the international market.

Enclave Economies

Local economic groups could not always—even with the limits referred to above—maintain control of production. In

---

sectors" entered the political game and threatened the established order.

certain circumstances, the economy of Latin American countries was incorporated into the world market through the output of economies controlled directly from abroad.

1. It appears that in most cases the formation of enclaves in the Latin American economies was a process in which nationally controlled economic sectors were gradually displaced because of their inability to compete in the production of commodities requiring technology, marketing systems, and heavy capital investment.[22]

2. The opposite extreme was the formation of enclaves as the direct result of expansion of the central economies; this occurred in countries where local groups had only been able to incorporate output marginally into the world market, which was the case in the continental Caribbean countries.

3. In the two cases, however, economic development based on enclaves came to express the vitality of the central economies and the nature of capitalism, irrespective of the activities of local groups. Also in both cases, although in different ways, enclave producers brought order to the national economic system and impressed upon it common characteristics. From the moment local output could no longer expand without foreign technology and capital,[23] or from the moment of its subordination to the international marketing systems, the activities of local producers began to lose significance in the development of the national economy. Local producers were thereby largely precluded from organizing an autonomous system of authority and resource allocation.

22. As was explained earlier, this type of production was based on direct capital formation, which was the only way a nationally controlled economy could develop. See Celso Furtado, *Development and Stagnation in Latin America: A Structural Approach* (New Haven: Yale University Press, 1965).

23. It should be recalled that national expansion depended basically on direct capital investment for the utilization of land and the available labor force.

The financial and commercial control that characterized European capitalism was replaced toward the end of the nineteenth century by investment oriented toward control of production in the peripheral world that was considered important for the central economies. Also in this period, the new world center of domination, the United States economy, because of its investment thrust and relative autonomy in many primary products, made it difficult for the Latin American economies tied to world trade through the United States market to expand as much as they had when they were linked to the European import system.

Incorporation of the Latin American export system into the world market through the creation of enclaves required Latin American countries to form a "modern sector" that was a kind of technological and financial extension of the central economies. Thus, the relative success of the export system was based on a highly specialized enclave economy with large surpluses. Growth of the export sector did not always create an internal market. It led to concentration of income in the enclave sector.

There have been both mining and plantation types of enclave. They differ in their respective technology, their use of labor, their levels of productivity, and the amount of capital investment required by each. Just as the plantation enclave employs much labor and may need little capital, the mining enclave uses little labor and needs a large capital input. In both cases, however, the enclave tends to worsen income distribution within the national economy. As production expands in the mining enclave, higher wages are paid to skilled labor without benefiting the sector of the economy oriented to the domestic market. When, on the other hand, the agricultural enclave expands and modernizes production, it takes over available land—affecting the subsistence economy and even the output for the domestic market—and it is not obliged to pay higher wages, because it uses more unskilled labor, which is usually abundant.

The enclave process took place in two separate situations of the Latin American economy. In one, an already existing national group lost control of the export sector and incorporated itself into the world market through the enclave. In the other, although enclaves coexisted with "traditional" oligarchies which controlled local economic sectors of little significance in the world market, the development of large-scale production was practically the direct result of the enclave. From a national standpoint, the problems in both cases were to define the bases and conditions for continuity of the local structure of domination and to determine the limits on the participation of its members in the new type of production represented by the enclaves. Also, in both cases, local political alliances had a double linkage: on the one hand, with the external sector of investment enterprises; on the other, internally, insofar as a group, by itself or allied with others, was able to establish a system of power and domination sufficiently strong and stable to negotiate with the external sector the terms on which economic exploitation of the enclaves would be accepted nationally, that is to say, accepted by oligarchic dominant sectors. The possibilities of relative autonomy of the internal vis-à-vis the external sectors differed in the two above-mentioned variants typical of the formation of enclaves.

The prior existence of a significant local export economy allowed the leading national groups to fall back upon other production sectors and to pursue a more aggressive policy with regard to concessions in the matter of taxes, compulsory reinvestment of profits, and so forth—all of which varied historically according to market conditions and the degree of political unity within the local dominant classes. Where only "traditional" oligarchies existed, they had little defense against the external sectors and were often transformed into groups patrimonially tied to the enclave economy insofar as national administration came to depend on the income generated by the externally controlled economic sector.

When national dominant groups could keep at least part control of production, national commercial and financial groups played a more prominent role by serving as a link with the external sector, while plantation and mine owners became less significant insofar as their economic action was limited to satisfying the demand of the domestic market. But it was frequently possible to orient sectors of the dominant classes toward activities that were more political and administrative than economic; for the alliances of groups often strengthened the regulating function of the state, thereby creating an important bureaucracy supported by the taxes collected from the enclave sector.

CHAPTER FOUR

Development and Social Change

The Political Role of Middle Classes

In Latin America, the economies that were integrated into the world market through enclaves or national control of export production expanded under the stimulus of external demand and attained some degree of economic diversification. At the same time, the structure of Latin American societies differentiated. New social groups grew up alongside those that were directly linked to the export economy, thereby adding new aspects to the confrontation of economic and political interests.

The export economies developed not only important financial and mercantile sectors, but also the initial stages of an urban-industrial society. Groups such as *latifundistas*, agricultural capitalists, mine owners, merchants, and bankers were all linked in varying ways to production. The changes that took place in the period we call "transition" show that the different relations among these groups in each country had strategic significance.

By "transition period" we mean the process by which diversification of the export economy led to the appearance of a middle class. The beginning of an industrial bourgeoisie with the corresponding technically trained professionals, the civil and military bureaucracy, the white-collar workers, and so forth depended on the way the export system was organized in each country. Nonetheless, the new social groups generally came into prominence during the first three decades of the twentieth century.

Latin American countries in which the national sector kept control of the export system developed social movements and a political life that differed from those of countries where the enclave economy finally prevailed in the phase of outward growth.

In some countries, local groups in charge of the economy reacted to enclave industries with a policy of withdrawing economically from the basic export sectors in order to retain control of other parts of the production system. At the same time, the rural or mercantile-financial bourgeoisie reached agreements with the enclave sector. In countries where the export system was weak, the policy of retrenchment and accommodation with international investment groups did not work, and the export sector became a mere agent of foreign enterprises. The economic scope of national enterprise was thereby limited to regional control of agricultural and mining output for the domestic market.

New and important differences were introduced into the enclave economy by the presence of British capitalism or the predominance of United States investment, as well as by the participation of the middle class in the game of power. These differences in turn influenced the first attempts by the Latin American countries to organize their economies by adding the stimulus of the domestic market to that of the external sector.

The economic transformation in the course of outward growth was produced by the slump in external demand due to moments of depression and reorientation of the world market. In the same way, the domestic output of products that were formerly imported was stimulated by the same factors and by the two world wars (1914–1918 and 1939–1945), as has been pointed out in numerous studies of industrialization in Latin America.

Politically, "oligarchic" domination in Latin America had begun to crumble before the 1929 world depression. The way in which the socio-political system was reorganized at this point depended on whether the socio-economic order was of the enclave type or of the type in which the local financial-agro-exporting bourgeoisie controlled production. In these two basic situations the internal differentiation of the social groups in each country of Latin America offered different outlooks for the formation—still channeled within the export system—of new alliances among the social groups. The varying success and possibilities of these alliances explain the persistence of the "constituted order" of exporting as well as the moment and the forms of transition from the "export system" to societies in which groups like the urban bourgeoisie and the "middle classes" linked to the domestic market became important.

A general outline will now be given to aid in an understanding of the social transformation that characterized the crisis of the oligarchic-export system.

The Transition Period in Societies with Production under National Control

The existence of an important "bourgeoisie" sector was a distinctive feature of societies where production was under national control. In this type of society, an expanding capitalist sector that organized output, part of marketing, and, in some countries, internal financing of the economy assured the formation of a national state. To establish a national order, the capitalist sector had to depend on a complex system of alliances with owners of low-productivity latifundia and with bureaucratic-military states, always bearing in mind that it owed its dominant position to its link with the external sector. In this type of country, a national bourgeoisie was created.[1]

The existence of this capitalist entrepreneurial sector, together with its alliances not only with the hacienda structure but also with external groups, is what determined structural possibilities in the transition period.

The crisis of this political system was brought on by pressure of the new social groups created by the export system. It varied according to the types of structures of domination that had been created by the export system; and to the diversification of output thanks to which an urban-industrial economy was slowly forming while parallel sectors were being developed within the export economy itself.

At least two specific situations can be distinguished in the process of domination in these countries:

1. In certain cases or periods, one of the "agro-commercial-exporting" sectors would set up the financial system and monopolize external relations through control of customs or through a strategic position in the external market, thereby asserting its dominance over not only the nation but especially the other producing groups. These were the conditions that most favored the appearance of an internal domination as the expression of a class situation. The dominant sector

1. The concept of bourgeoisie in this context acquires a meaning that is historically different from that of the European bourgeoisie, for one reason because the role of the city as a base of political power and a center of economic activity was not the same in the two situations. Here this concept is used to stress the character of "capitalist producers" or "capitalist entrepreneurs"—linked mostly with the rural area—as opposed to the concept of rural patriciate, feudal groups, or landed oligarchy. Although the latter played an important role in these countries, they were always subordinate to the capitalist entrepreneurs; it should also be pointed out that the concepts of seigniory or feudalism are inadequate to describe them.

of the export system became the bourgeoisie, which imposed its own order on the rest of the elite, thereby exhibiting a "class unity," in which it maintained—although without eliminating conflicts—the interests of the remaining groups that made up the "dominant class": the regional bourgeoisie and the latifundistas with their related bureaucratic sectors. An example of this was the dominant position of the Buenos Aires bourgeoisie in Argentina.

2. In other cases, the leading sector could not achieve the "class unity" it needed in order to appear as the undisputed representative of a single system of domination. In this situation lack of a clearly hegemonic group within the dominant class led to a confederation or tacit agreement among the various agro-exporting groups. Even though such confederations did not establish a system of alternate succession for control of the state—for one particular sector might have sufficient strength to formally control the central mechanisms of power—they did define the sphere of internal influence of the state, thereby safeguarding the autonomy of the provincial centers of power. In this situation, there was bound to be a power struggle among the capitalist-exporting groups, permitting other components of the alliances of power to gain ground. National or regional domination was assured only by a more active participation of the latifundistas and the local bourgeoisie, and even of the military and bureaucratic estates linked to them. Therefore, in situations of this kind and contrary to that described above, the oligarchic-latifundista group seemed to dominate, and this appearance disguised the capitalist-bourgeois character of the system of domination, as was the case in Brazil before 1930.

In special and limiting cases, these two situations might be more clear-cut. In the first, the export sector[2] could establish an effective "class monopoly" thanks to the weakness of the differentiated sectors within the alliance of domina-

2. Export sector will be taken to mean in this chapter the group composed of plantation, livestock, and mine owners as well as

tion. Its force of expansion either eclipsed all the other sectors or placed them in a position of subordination rather than alliance. Because in Latin America this situation occurred precisely in the countries with the weakest economies, such a "class monopoly" did not indicate a vigorous bourgeoisie. Actually, it was based on the agro-export sector controlled by large landholders who, therefore, combined the characteristics of the oligarchic-latifundista group with those of the capitalist-exporting group. This was especially true in Central America where, moreover, the increasing subordination of the economy to the enclave system prevented countries from having a national policy of their own.

In the second situation—that of the power struggle between various groups of the dominant class—a "balance" was reached through an explicit agreement as to the internal division of spheres of influence. In this case, the nation was represented by the state fundamentally in its external relations; for within the country the administrative cadres of the opposing "parties" made up a state bureaucracy through a sectorial or regional division of spheres of influence within the state apparatus. This situation occurred in Latin America, not only in countries where the power struggle led to an alliance in which the oligarchic-latifundista groups were very important (the Liberal and Conservative parties of Colombia), but also in countries like Uruguay, which had two forms of domination, one of which—the Colorado party with its active capitalist-exporting group—approximated the first-mentioned situation where "class unity" was maintained under a clearly bourgeois group.

The degree of diversification of national production also affected the transition that interests us here. Three different economic situations affected the formation of new social

---

merchants oriented to the external market. In each country, one or another of the production types prevailed according to the relative importance of agriculture, livestock, or mining in the economy.

groups and the consolidation of domination in countries that controlled their own production.

1. The export system was composed of a single product, and there was no diversification of output through production for the domestic market, as in Central America.

2. In an export system with little or no diversification, sectors of production for the domestic market were created or maintained, as in Uruguay and Argentina before the boom in cereals.

3. The export system was diversified, giving rise to export sectors parallel to the main product and also making possible the formation of a sector of production directed to the domestic market, as in Brazil.[3]

Our analysis does not consider the foregoing information to be determinant of the structural possibilities for social change. Our own interpretation stresses the need to know how the system of domination was constituted, starting from these economic conditions and bearing in mind that the presence or absence of parallel export sectors could have been the result of domination by a group that controlled the rest of the system either directly or through a "confederation" of exporting groups that controlled output.

The presence or absence of parallel export sectors affected internal diversification of the economy through the social division of labor. It affected not only the domestic market structure but also the creation of new social groups. These social groups were not just the mechanical result of an "economic structure"; they tried to develop or modify that structure as a means of imposing or maintaining their particular form of domination.

The dominant exporting group might have gained control of national output by imposing a single-commodity

3. We have described given historical situations rather than theoretical possibilities of paired combinations, as would be present in a formal analysis and would require a far more complete "typology."

economy, or it might have had to ally itself with other regional exporting groups. A single exporting group could more easily achieve domination in small countries, where the nation could emerge as the result of the action of one dominant homogeneous socio-economic group, than in large countries, where the limits of national production had to be set in terms of regional alliances. Nevertheless, it can be said that usually a dominant agro-exporting group tried to exercise monopoly through a system of single-commodity production which assured it almost absolute political control.

Economically, size determined whether or not the export system made possible the formation of a production sector for the domestic market. The diversified export economies that reached a certain size through the creation of parallel export sectors necessarily helped form production sectors directed to the domestic market. The change from a purely export economy to one that produced output for the domestic market reflected the growth of that economy. Expansion of the export economy encouraged domestic demand because it required an agricultural industry and because, in any event, the complexity of export production developed new domestic consumers. Since rural labor had a very low capacity for consumption, it was not the number but the social division of the labor employed in agricultural output that contributed to internal demand. It was the capitalist development of agriculture[4] which compelled the "hacienda" to introduce some specialization into its production and to break up the traditional organization of its labor that had made it a self-sufficient economic unit. This provided urban centers with a larger market for their economic activities, and the new social

---

4. Expanded consumption, insofar as it contributed significantly to formation of a domestic market, was limited to consumption by the producers themselves, who had become capitalists. It was also linked to the emergence of new urban centers—that is, new markets—created by the capitalization of agriculture and the consequent decline of the hacienda.

groups emerged in the cities: craftsmen, tradesmen, professionals, and the service sector comprising transportation, banking, education, public utilities, and·so forth. The urban-industrial social groups, composed of an urban bourgeoisie and a working class, initially grew out of expansion of the export sector and were identified with its interests.

These historical-structural conditions explain the formation of the urban-industrial groups and the degree of internal social differentiation produced by expansion of the export economy. The growth of these forces, however, depended on the unity and differentiation of the agro-exporting groups and on the alliances between some of these groups and the emerging social sectors. In countries where the dominant groups united and established a monopoly of power, the crisis of the system of oligarchic domination did not have the same consequences as in countries where such unity did not exist and non-dominant groups in the agro-export sector became allied with emerging social groups to set up a new and broader social scheme of political leadership. In the latter countries, the new social groups, thanks to their participation in the state, were able to make alliances with those sectors of the oligarchic-exporting groups that sought the economic support of public investment.

There will follow a brief discussion of attempts by the middle classes to enter the alliances of power.

INCORPORATION OF THE MIDDLE CLASSES INTO THE HEGEMONY OF THE EXPORTING BOURGEOISIE: THE CASE OF ARGENTINA

The development of the agricultural and livestock exports in Argentina also expanded production tied to the domestic market and—given the political domination of Buenos Aires—especially encouraged urban growth.[5] Consequently,

5. In 1869 the population of Argentina was 1,727,076, in 1895 it was 3,954,911, and in 1914 it was 7,885,327, having increased 127.7 percent in the first period and 99.4 percent in the second. "Urban growth reached its medium intensity between 1895 and

the dynamism of the "outward development" (export) of the Argentine economy generated a social differentiation of groups into "middle sectors" such as those linked to government administration (both civil and military), professional groups, the sectors linked to the administration and control of export enterprises, and even those linked to the industries and services oriented toward the domestic market.

It is clear that the new social groups, on the political level, and the businesses and activities oriented toward the domestic market, on the economic level, were subordinates to the agro-exporting groups and businesses linked to the export economy. In particular, the local bourgeoisie, the landholders who owned low-productivity latifundia, and the immigrant wheat farmers of the littoral provinces were socially and politically subordinate to the exporting groups just as were the agrarian, mercantile, and industrial bourgeoisie of the interior provinces. The various groups could be joined under the hegemony of the agro-livestock-exporting sector insofar as the latter's domination through the state apparatus appeared to express the unity of the dominant sectors.

This process began when Rosas was overthrown in 1852, and it was consolidated with the policy of President Roca after 1880. On the political-ideological level it took the form of a struggle between centralism (that is, national political unification) and federalism. The livestock-exporting groups of Buenos Aires, which had advocated federalism as a way of imposing their interests on the other provinces, ended by accepting the 1853 constitution of the Argentine Confederation. This constitution was the work of Alberdi, who came from the interior province of Tucumán and belonged to the liberal generation of 1837, and it expressed the new political

---

1914. In this period the urbanization index rose 0.77 per annum, whereas in the previous period it had gone up 0.43." Gustavo Beyhaut, quoted by Roberto Corte Conde in "Problemas del crecimiento industrial de la Argentina, 1870–1914," *Desarrollo Económico* (Buenos Aires), vol. 3, no. 12 (April–September), pp. 156–157.

reality: an authoritarian centralism. It agreed to a division of
the spheres of influence among the provinces or, more precisely, among the local caudillos, as well as to acquisition of
property through annexation of Indian lands and to labor
through immigration. These were the bases of the ideology
held in common by the dominant groups. When Mitre, the
governor of Buenos Aires Province, was elected president of
the Confederation in 1862, Buenos Aires was accepted "cen-
tralistically" as the politically hegemonic force of the nation.
(There was a brief period of rule by Urquiza, the governor
of Entre Ríos who had expelled Rosas in 1852 and occupied
Buenos Aires in alliance with Uruguayan caudillos and who
was supported by Brazil and by the French-English interests
opposed to the Rosas policy of excluding foreign trade from
the Paraná River.)

Meanwhile, important changes had reintegrated the Latin American economy into world trade and given it a new
impulse. The economic expansion which proceeded almost
unbrokenly from the 1850s until the crisis of 1873 favored
the emergence of new social groups in the River Plate region.
The political targets after Roca continued to be oriented
toward exports, immigration, investment by foreign capital,
and foreign loans to the provinces and to the nation. The
1880s were a period of expansion and of moderate progress in
secularization. The political system operated under the oligarchic control of Buenos Aires, in the sense that exporting
interests predominated, without broad political participation,
much less a representative system guaranteed by free elections.[6]

Politically, this lack of participation gave rise to a new
opposition involving a complicated alliance, which included
the urban middle classes of the littoral provinces, especially

6. In fact, both Roca and, subsequently, the Celman government encouraged secularization and regional integration at the
level of national power, replacing regional courts with another,
more integrated system. This political modernization, however,
did not bring about a representative electoral system.

Buenos Aires; the rural middle class composed of the immigrant wheat farmers; the cattle ranchers who were not connected with the feeders and meat packers; and even those sectors of the upper classes of the interior provinces that had been pushed aside by the way in which the Confederation was politically dominated by the Buenos Aires elite.

The political activities of the new classes and the marginal groups of the old dominant classes began in the very heart of the oligarchic system with an uprising against President Juárez Celman in 1890. Although the insurrection was crushed, Celman resigned in favor of Vice-President Carlos Pellegrini. This marked the beginning of the radical sector of civil opposition, the Unión Cívica Radical (the Radical Civic Union).[7]

The pressure of the new groups was aimed at participating in the alliance of power in order to reestablish "public morality" and to broaden the bases of power. In addition to this program, the new groups also advocated federalism, which meant greater participation of the once prosperous provinces, now left out of the system of national decisions.

Having no access to the oligarchic political system, the opposition moved from reformism to rebellion, by which they tried and failed to gain power in 1893 and 1904. Once more the system triumphed over internal divisions. Mitre, again a candidate, this time for "national union," riding the wave of "broader participation," was ousted from the political game by Roca, who had retained control of the "situationalist" bloc and who preferred to continue with the conservative domination based on fraudulent elections. This policy, which depended on an alliance with provincial officialdom, was less and less responsive to mass pressures, that

7. See Silvia Sigal and Ezequiel Gallo, "La formación de los partidos contemporáneos: la Unión Cívica Radical, 1880–1916," *Desarrollo Económico*, vol. 1, special number on Latin America (April–September 1963), pp. 173–230. The above outline of radicalism, and other points as well, are based on this article.

is, from the new groups already described plus the urban workers who were coming under the influence of anarcho-syndicalism, until 1912 when President Sáenz Pena agreed to promulgate the electoral law that was to bear his name, which assured universal suffrage and free elections. In this way, the head of Unión Cívica Radical, Hipólito Irigoyen, was elected to the presidency.

The election of Irigoyen signified the victory of an alliance of power in which the electoral base differed significantly from the elite directing it. This elite was composed of the class sectors marginalized by the previous dominant system: the farmers of the Littoral provinces—Sante Fe, Córdoba, Entre Ríos—who, with the expansion of world trade, had increased output and intensified immigration; the groups connected with the more traditional agro-livestock production and trade who had not participated in the dominant political scheme; and finally, the middle classes—both the bureaucratic and those created by the growth of services and commerce in cities that were multiplying because of the spread of agricultural production. The economic and social differentiation of Buenos Aires also added to the weight of the middle class.

The burgeoning radicalism was largely incorporated into the alliances of power of the marginalized sectors of the traditional classes and of the classes that had never been dominant but that gained power with the increase in the cereal production of the Littoral and with the expansion of the export economy near the end of the century. But radicalism in 1961 also expressed a pact between the middle sectors and the dominant classes. The nature of the radical program indicated that the groups making up the Unión Cívica Radical were not united "on the basis of similar social and economic problems, but that their only common denominator was their exclusion from political power."[8] Consequently, it was easy

8. Sigal and Gallo, *op. cit.*, p. 184.

to extend the alliance "upward" to incorporate the economic demands of the agricultural sectors, the livestock owners, and the exporters.[9]

In any case, the radical policy, thanks to its ability to mobilize votes, united in the system of power sectors of the middle classes and of the urban popular strata, to which were added the regional agro-exporting and urban-industrial groups. The peculiar features of the radical program permitted the government also to include representatives of the old dominant strata, which remained strong enough to react against the rising pressures from below. When there was a strike of workers of meat-packing plants, the radical government used the navy in support of the foreign meat-packing interests, even though the latter were opposed nationally by the cattle ranchers.

Taking advantage of the adverse effects of the economic crisis of 1918 on the radical government, the agro-livestock exporting sector proposed, to the national agrarian bourgeoisie supporting it and to the urban bourgeoisie frightened by the popular movement, a new, more gradual scheme of transition for production interests. This policy began as a reaction against the student protests that culminated in the University Reform of Córdoba and against the workers led by the Federación Obrera Regional Argentina (the Regional Federation of Argentine Workers), which was strongly influenced by anarcho-syndicalism. It was during the "tragic week" of 1919 that the Irigoyen government violently put down the urban pressures.

Irigoyenismo, which attracted the votes of the masses but did not direct them through the labor union apparatus,

9. See the article by Peter Smith, "Los radicales argentinos y la defensa de los intereses ganaderos, 1916–1930," *Desarrollo Económico,* vol. 7, no. 25 (April–June 1967), pp. 795–830, which shows the participation of cattle ranchers, farmers, and exporters in the radical governments. This participation decreased in the second government of Irigoyen, 1928–1930.

was replaced in the Unión Cívica Radical by a non-personalist (that is, non-populist) radicalism that elected Marcelo de Alvear to the presidency in 1922. The new policy reassured the elite members of the radical alliance by rejecting the Irigoyen model of broadened political participation, which had mobilized the masses without controlling them.

Social and economic groups were integrated into the new agreement as follows: an important role was given to those who acted in the national sphere as representatives of foreign interests, especially of the British, and who linked both the Argentine state and the national economy with the external sectors; the national exporting bourgeoisie was restored to its leading role in the government either directly or through representatives. This successful counteroffensive was aided by the economic fact of the prosperity of the export system. The middle classes and urban bourgeoisie did not have to risk coming out in favor of an economic policy that would make them independent of the agro-exporting bourgeoisie as long as the old export system functioned satisfactorily.

It is nonetheless significant that Irigoyen tried to lay the foundation for this independence. He created the government-owned petroleum corporation, Yacimientos Petrolíferos Fiscales, he tried to nationalize the railroads, and he took advantage of the favorable conditions brought about by World War I to expand the textile and metallurgical industries. Succeeding Alvear, Irigoyen was returned to the presidency in 1928 by the combined support of the "radicals" and certain sectors of the regional dominant groups, principally the wine producers of Mendoza and San Juan. But the unity of the agro-export establishment again broke up the alliance attempted by the Irigoyen government, which was further weakened by its failure to control the political threat of labor unions dissatisfied over an economic policy that favored the bourgeoisie by promoting the domestic market.

Following the military coup of Uriburu in 1930, there was an alliance of "Conservatives," "Anti-Personalists," and "Independent Socialists," which represented "transition" in that the system of power was opened to modernization. However, it rejected alliance with the new groups when these seemed to express popular movements, and it defended itself by appealing to military intervention and to "patriotism." It did this until the pressure of the middle classes was augmented by that of the popular movement (*Peronismo*).

INCORPORATION OF THE "TRADITIONAL" MIDDLE CLASSES AND THE CRISIS OF OLIGARCHIC-BOURGEOIS DOMINATION: BRAZIL

The transition period revealed the weakness of class structure in Brazil. Brazil's export economy was first moved toward a full capitalist path through the abolition of slavery and then through the fall of the Empire. The Empire was a symbolic but also an effective guarantee of regional interests based on a slave economy and a patrimonialist domination. Until 1860–1870, the sugar interests of the Northeast and the coffee growers of the center of the country (Minas Gerais, the province of Rio de Janeiro, and the neighboring part of São Paulo in the Paraíba Basin) prevailed politically in the game of regional alliances. There was respect for, as well as conflict with, the local interests of the slaveholders who owned large properties in the south and the Northeast as well as in the provinces marginal to the center of power. The Empire organized a politically skilled and socially important bureaucracy that, thanks to the moderating influence of the emperor, not only safeguarded the local autonomy of the seigniorial planters but also preserved the national state. The state watched over "general interests," that is, the sugar and coffee producers, on condition that the latter maintain and respect local centers of power.

Oligarchic domination was politically effective but always made political bargains in the name of the interests of the national state. The formal political game between the two parties—one liberal and the other conservative—permitted the very groups that belonged to the dominant oligarchy to attempt to introduce progressive political thought from

Europe or North America. It would be a mistake to under-estimate the political importance of these "progressive" currents, because they seem to be so far removed from the national reality of a slave-labor society. The transition in the system of political control was largely determined by noncon-formist groups within the oligarchy.

A pure capitalist situation crystallized for the first time in the "agro-export system" when the coffee growers of São Paulo began to replace slaves with immigrant labor, chiefly after 1870. The breakdown of the slave system and then the fall of the Empire (1889) expressed that new reality, just as it also indicated the solidarity of "traditional urban middle class" groups with the farmers (*fazendeiros*).

In a plantation and slave-labor economy, the process of social division of labor was and had to be slight. Although the introduction of free labor into the coffee economy meant a greater division of labor and reinforcement of the urban economy, this process did not significantly affect social mo-bility until about World War I. Nonetheless, the pressures of the new social groups had been in evidence since the per-iod of Abolition (1888) and the Republic (1889). Initially, these pressures were exerted through groups that were of secondary importance within the traditional oligarchic strata. They belonged to the civil and principally military bureau-cracies (the latter was strengthened after the 1865–1870 war with Paraguay), or they played a subordinate role as lawyers, congressmen, party wheels, and local leaders of less wealthy provinces.

In the abolition of slavery and the formation of the Re-public, these sectors, which only very loosely could be called middle, joined the coffee growers of São Paulo and some non-slaveholding producers of the south in order to displace the imperial oligarchy. At first there was even an anti-oli-garchic radicalization. But this was soon stifled by the estab-lishment of the federalist republican form of government under the Constitution of 1891. This constitution expressed the system of local alliances under the domination of the agro-exporting capitalists of the center-south, but it did not exclude the agro-exporting groups of other regions, still less the owners of large low-productivity estates. These last, because of their substantial number, were able to place a traditional stamp on the system, even though the latter actually had been in the hands of the capitalist producers and exporters of the center-south since the nineteenth century.

The gradual differentiation in the urban economy, which was speeded up by World War I, added as urban protagonists professionals, government and white-collar workers, and some sectors of the working class—who gave a new meaning to the anti-oligarchic reaction. Nevertheless, even in the 1920s, this reaction continued to be expressed through young military men whose behavior and ideology could only be explained in terms of the earlier anti-oligarchic reaction that had originated in the marginal and economically declining sectors of the regional oligarchies themselves.

The shakiness of the oligarchic-capitalist domination, which had been based on regional alliances exclusively among the dominant groups, became apparent with the 1930 revolution. The breakdown began with clashes between the oligarchic groups themselves over control of national power. When some of the regional groups of domination broadened the scheme of political alliances to reinforce themselves against the nationally dominant oligarchies, they opened the way to the new urban groups. The latter immediately began to harass the dominant sector of the old oligarchic alliance— the coffee growers of São Paulo and Minas Gerais—until a new agreement on the control of power was reached.

Actually, the liberal alliance of Vargas represented the interests of regional groups like the ranch owners in the south and sugar-plantation owners in the Northeast, with whom the "urban middle sectors" had come to an understanding against the dominant coffee-growers, who had been weakened by the 1929 world depression. The old dominant groups naturally opposed this new alliance, but they were unsuccessful and became politically isolated and economically weakened.

The policy of Vargas later strengthened the urban middle class and small sectors of the popular class without putting economic obstacles in the way of the agro-export sector. A few years later, Vargas tried to recover support of the earlier dominant sectors, including the coffee growers, in order to establish a new alliance of power, which, even if it excluded the peasant farmer, slowly incorporated the urban popular sectors. His policy maintained the level of employment and, thereby, also the domestic market and national industry. It did this through heavy public investment in infrastructure and through increased government controls.

The old oligarchic-capitalist alliance was replaced by a centralist policy that respected local agro-exporting interests, but created the necessary urban economic base for an industrial and mercantile bourgeoisie. This aided the differentiation of social structure by creating a new "middle class" and the expanding working class.

In the first Vargas government of 1930–1949 there was no real participation of the worker-popular sectors in the alliances of power. It is true that from the time he ran for office in 1930, Vargas insisted on the importance of industrial expansion, especially in iron and steel, and he embarked on a nationalist, corporative program. But it should not be forgotten that these two policies followed worldwide trends. The presence of oligarchic delegates in the Constituent Congress of 1934, the drafting of the Mining Code in 1934, and the creation of the National Council of Petroleum in 1938 were also part of the international scenes foreshadowing the world war: the need for an autarchic national economy and the idea of a corporative state. The policy of Vargas during that period with regard to supporting the price of coffee, maintaining the level of employment, and strengthening the industrial sector oriented toward the domestic market was more an ad hoc response to market conditions than an attempt to change the economic bases of the system of power. But these economic bases came to include, instead of the ousted oligarchic sector, representatives of the urban middle groups and of the mercantile and industrial bourgeoisie.

The attempt in 1935 by the National Liberation Alliance (the radical urban middle class, both civil and military, and the Communist party) to broaden the political scheme "downward" was followed by the coup d'etat that created the Estado Novo (New State) in 1937, which culminated a period of repression. Subsequently, the ambiguous policy of Vargas was to harry the conservative political interests and at the same time offer them participation. Thus, he declared the fascist Integralista party to be illegal after he had accepted its tacit support; he used the representatives of the bourgeoisie of São Paulo and Minas Gerais to initiate and maintain a policy of repression; and he offered government posts to his old enemies in the defeated oligarchies. Although in this process he was far removed from the concerns of the working class, he continued and intensified the nationalist policy favoring industrialization (the state-controlled Volta Redonda steel mill was the first industrial plant in this strategic sector), and he encouraged an active policy of industrialization through the misnamed Foreign Trade Council.

After 1943, when Vargas consolidated an advanced labor code, he redefined his policy. Brazil's worker organizations, like those of Argentina and Chile, had been founded at the turn of the century under the influence of European-style anarchists and syndicalists. They were abolished during the first Vargas period and revived under state direction. In their revived form they incorporated a new proletariat. The original São Paulo workers, who had been mainly Italian immigrants, were replaced after the industrialization of the 1930s by other workers who were national migrants and entered the political scene under state tutelage.

There was still no participation of the masses. The political process had incorporated into the alliances of power no more than a few sectors of the middle class. While some of these were oriented toward production for the domestic market, they all still excluded the masses from the centers of decision-making.

INCORPORATION OF THE MIDDLE CLASS INTO THE
ALLIANCE FOR POWER: THE DEMOCRATIZATION
OF URUGUAY

The economic structure of Uruguay was oriented to export and included two important groups: the hacendados, who actually controlled production; and the merchants, who were most directly linked to export activity. These sectors were so bound together that it was not unusual for merchants to become ranch owners and ranch owners to become merchants. Precisely because of this connection, the two groups often competed for political power and tried to encroach on each other's economic domain.

The structure of the traditional parties, Blancos and Colorados, was largely determined by the relationship described above. Membership in the two parties was similar, but in the Blanco party ranchers were more important than merchants, and in the Colorado party the reverse was true. This meant that although both parties were economically oriented to export, the Blancos defended the production sector of the economy, which was the hacienda, and the Colorados were concerned with marketing and therefore with outward development.

The struggle for power produced frequent political crises that were interrupted only when the military government of Latorre (1876–1880) took steps to create a more stable political alliance between the two parties. Colorado and Blanco figures, none really outstanding, alternated in the Latorre government; this was the period when economic interests began to be expressed through the Farmers' Association and the Chamber of Commerce. During the Latorre government, growth of the export economy was stimulated by even closer ties to Great Britain. At the same time, a more advanced rural technology was incorporated (barbed-wire fences, scientific cattle breeding, etc.), and immigration from Europe was encouraged. These factors, which accelerated the social division of labor, also contributed to urbanization and to a greater complexity in social stratification.

It was not long before middle and popular groups began to acquire political importance. They became the axis of the Batlle policy with its program of economic, political, and social change. In practice, the social composition of the parties was not substantially altered. Batlle first attempted to gain control of the Colorado party by incorporating and enlisting the support of the urban middle and popular classes as well as the farmers. His next objective was control of the state, but for this he had to mobilize not only the popular and middle groups but the entire party with its complex structure of social groups. This "power," if we can call it that, was precarious. After becoming president of the republic in 1903, Batlle applied to the state the policy by which he formerly had controlled the Colorado party. He restructured the state apparatus and turned its bureaucracy over to the social sectors that had supported him.

The policy of Batlle went farther, however. Returning to the tradition of Varela, who under Latorre had organized secular education, he increased the number of schools. He modernized political institutions and, especially in his second presidential period after 1911, adopted measures for "social democracy." His labor reforms established old-age and retirement pensions and encouraged the expansion of trade unions. Perhaps even more significant was his economic policy, which included protectionism and an attempt to create marketing and insurance monopolies.

After 1920 he launched a transport program that liberated the country from English railway interests. It is clear that a change of this magnitude involved something more than a struggle between the alliance of the middle sectors and the agrarian bourgeoisie: as Uruguay loosened its ties with Great Britain, it became increasingly dependent on the United

States, which involved an important change in economic terms.

The Constitution of 1917 opened the doors of political decision to the new sectors incorporated by the Batlle policy. Batlle controlled the party because he had incorporated into it the middle class and some popular groups, but he could not expel the other sectors from the party. He had won a political victory through the party structure, but he could not altogether dislodge the Blancos from real power. In 1919 the Constitutional Assembly accepted the part of the Batlle proposal that created the collegial executive. From that time, the Blanco minority had a voice in administrative decisions, even though political and military functions were reserved to the president. Subsequent political stability, therefore, was due not to a monopoly of power by a social group or sector, but to a complex system of alliances and spheres of power. The alliance was expressed in a state economic policy (nationalization, creation of fiscal enterprises, social services, etc.) that did not disregard class interests or favor one group to the detriment of others.

THE OLIGARCHIC DOMINATION AND THE WEAKNESS
OF THE MIDDLE CLASS: COLOMBIA

Colombian politics also revealed a continual struggle among sectors of the dominant class and among the commercial and exporting groups with their respective plantation dependencies. It would be a mistake to think that the struggle between Liberal and Conservative in the nineteenth century expressed a conflict between landed gentry and bourgeois capitalists. The Conservative party was supported by families of aristocratic lineage and also by the merchants and plantation owners from Antioquia, who are usually credited with having played an important part in modernizing Colombian production. In the nineteenth century, the Liberals included groups that represented the two faces of the country: the large landholders of the colonial patrimonialist past and the progressive exporters of the tobacco and coffee economy, as well as groups of merchants.

In spite of the violence of the political struggle, a flourishing agro-exporting bourgeoisie managed throughout to impose temporary compromises among the factions. Conservative catholicism and liberal agnosticism alike yielded to the efficiency and dynamism of a plutocracy that was beginning to develop an industrial economy. Under the Liberal Rafael Núñez, the Constitution of 1886 expressed the explicit pact of power between the two ideological extremes of the same class.

The career of Rafael Núñez illustrates this process. The Liberal tradition, which was the most radical, especially during the administration of President Mosquera, supported free trade, expulsion of the Jesuits, religious liberty, abolition of slavery, and federalism. Núñez began as a member of the most extreme faction, called *golgota,* of the Liberals. When he became president in 1880, he changed his position to progressive pragmatism. He believed that it was necessary to check the disruption of provincial life by violent local politics that federalism led to. To do this, he thought, the power of the presidency had to be strengthened. At the same time, by incorporating the above-mentioned producers and merchants, the Núñez government came to represent order and progress; and from then on it not only expressed but commanded Colombian conservatism.

Thus, a political arrangement was made in Colombia that embraced all the dominant class, from its most backward to its most economically progressive groups, and it even managed to include the rural and provincial middle sectors.

All subsequent attempts at reaction, although internal to the system of power, were violent (1884–1885; 1895; 1899–1903—the Thousand-Day War), and they all failed. Internal politics continued to deteriorate until there was a breakdown in the national structure of the country, which culminated in the secession of the Isthmus of Panama in 1903.

At the beginning of the twentieth century, the industrial economy recovered thanks to investment in the domestic market by the bourgeois sectors. This not only encouraged urban growth in the first quarter of the century, but also accelerated social differentiation. The "petite bourgeoisie" expanded, and urban and agricultural working classes emerged as a result of industrialization and of foreign exploitation of petroleum and banana resources.

For the first time, and in spite of the "oligarchic pact" —which was made and unmade according to the caprice of the political interests but which was maintained vis-à-vis the other classes—the political presence of other classes made itself known. It remained an indirect "presence" that echoed "liberalizing" sectors of the dominant classes. But popular protest grew along with economic prosperity. It was intensified by the indemnity obtained from Panama, and reached its peak just before the world depression. The labor strikes and protests of the workers of the United Fruit Company and of the Tropical Oil Company were often and violently repressed. But they signalled the dawning complexity of Colombian politics and social structure.

The political polarization that reflected the new differentiation of society first occurred under Rafael Uribe within the Liberal party itself. Almost all the socialist leaders of the 1920s came from the dominant classes, and were later reabsorbed by the bipartisan game. Only when there was political fragmentation in the dominant classes could groups that did not belong to these sectors participate in the struggle for power. Typically and tragically, Eliécer Gaitán, head of the left wing of the Liberal party, who won widespread support among the urban workers and who was assassinated in 1948, was to symbolize this situation. The urban middle and popular classes tried every avenue of protest from criticism of the constituted order to a violent and frustrated attempt to destroy it, having sought and failed to reform from within. The limited differentiation within social groups, and the monolithic character of the oligarchic-bourgeois classes, blocked

access of the middle groups to power and helped maintain
the oligarchic pact. Yet this political immobilization did not
lead to economic stagnation. Therefore, unlike development
in countries in which pressure from middle and popular sectors could be exercised within the political system, development in Colombia was produced and directed by the bourgeois
sector that managed the "national front."

ECONOMIC CRISIS, POLITICAL CRISIS, AND INDUSTRIALIZATION

The various historical-structural conditions briefly re-
viewed here explain why in some countries the agro-export
political system remained stable, in spite of the 1929 depression, and why in others the established order was altered.
And it also explains the different traits and durations of the
historical transition in countries where the emergence of urban-industrial sectors added to the difficulties of the transition period. The continuation of the oligarchic-export system
in countries like Colombia even after 1929 and until the end
of World War II becomes understandable when we consider
that there was no significant diversification of the export system and that no important sector of production was developed for the domestic market.

On the other hand, comparative analysis of the political
crises in Argentina and Brazil makes evident the differences
in the situations of the two countries. In Brazil, although the
groups engendered by the urban-industrial expansion of the
epoch were weaker than in Argentina, it is also true that the
unity of the dominant classes was more fragile. When the
possibility arose of a political transition benefiting the non-
oligarchic-exporting groups, worker-popular pressure lacked
the force it had gathered in Argentina.

The interpretations here presented therefore stress the
political conditions that favored measures to strengthen the
domestic market. In keeping with the methodological in-
spiration of our work, they also emphasize that the factors

"explaining" the type of development carried out in the various countries were social differentiation and, correlatively, the balance of power among the social groups, rather than just the diversification of the economy during the period of outward expansion. Our interpretation of course recognizes that economic factors played an important role in the new type of development characterized by industrialization and the formation of a domestic market. Some of these factors have already been mentioned in this chapter and include the disruption of the world market, the protection of employment from the crisis in the export economy, and the interruption by World War I of the traditional flow of imports but not of corresponding magnitudes of exports.

In some countries, the agro-exporting groups managed to weather the 1929 depression by simply adopting classic economic measures: in Argentina, a corporate organization of export interests by the government; in Central America, an orthodox monetary policy to maintain the gold value of currency even at the price of unemployment. Once the slump in the world market was over, the agro-exporting groups believed they could become prosperous through formation of an industrial sector, although only as a supplementary resource, and through a limited expansion of the domestic market. The problem is to explain the reasons that prompted them in their choice of alternatives.

Our hypothesis states that development changed fundamentally in character after the 1929 depression as a result of pressure on the political system by new social groups and of the reaction by groups linked to the export sector. Thus, the political consequences of the world depression depended on the prevailing scheme of domination in each country. In some cases, the crisis signified only a strengthening of the oligarchic domination, often in military forms in order to deal with the unrest produced by the restrictive monetary policy that lowered the capacity of the production sector to absorb labor. This occurred in Argentina, where the agro-exporting groups took advantage of the effects of the 1929 depression to consolidate their domination, if only temporarily.

It is also true that the agro-exporting groups lost much of their privileged position to direct representatives of the capitalism of the central countries.

Where oligarchic domination could be broadened to include more classes, the transformation of development was intensified. In such cases, it appeared that the economic crisis, which preceded industrialization, had been the cause of the consolidation of the domestic market and of the concomitant partial breakdown in oligarchic domination. Indeed, this was precisely the theory behind industrialist ideology.

In reality, history was not so mechanical, even in the most industrialized countries. The dominant social groups allied themselves and worked together after the world depression to impose their own system of domination and to organize production. In the Latin American countries that industrialized, as well as in those that did not and had a corresponding increase in the relative importance of their export economy, the different courses taken by development depended on the way in which the social classes—"traditional" or new—activated their force. The level of complexity that was reached in the social division of work by a country during the period of outward expansion also affected development, because it placed structural limitations on the emergence of new social groups and on their possibilities of action.

If we compare the diversification of Argentina production during the 1930s and of Brazilian production during the same period we can clearly see that economic differences were secondary in policies of industrial development and formation of a domestic market. Although Argentina initially made more progress in its structure of production, by the 1930s its industrial policy was less effective than that of Brazil. Thanks to Brazil's socio-political scheme, a domestic market was formed a decade earlier than in Argentina.

The Enclave Economies in the Period of Transition

History followed another direction in countries where economic activity was ordered by an enclave. Here it is necessary to take into account not only the diversities due to the type of enclave—mining or agricultural—but also the degree of diversification in the national sector of the economy as well as the political process through which the groups controlling that sector organized the state and defined their relations with each other, with subordinate classes, and with the external groups that made up the economic enclaves.

"Enclaves" were fixed into the Latin American economy between the end of the nineteenth century and the beginning of the twentieth, when national political groups already had power and controlled important economic sectors. As in the preceding cases, the dynamics of transition assumed different forms according to how diversified production was in each country, which determined the structural possibilities of action for the various classes and groups. In countries with an enclave economy, the structure of domination was a direct manifestation of the political subordination of the worker and peasant sectors to the dominant classes; whereas in countries where national producers predominated, domination was more economic than political.

In enclave situations, economic exploitation was effected politically. The national dominant groups were linked to foreign enterprises more as a politically dominant class than as an "entrepreneurial sector," and it was the foreign enterprises that established direct economic relations with the worker and peasant classes. The economic weakness of national groups of power obliged these groups to maintain a more exclusive form of domination, because they could remain in power only through their connection with the enclave sector, which depended on their ability to keep an internal order that would ensure the supply of labor and natural resources needed by the enclave for economic exploitation.

These same circumstances meant that workers and peasants, although excluded from the political game, were concentrated in centers of potential protest. The middle sectors found incorporation more difficult because they would have to use the "under class" as shock troops to breach the exclusive political system, and this could shake up the *entire* structure of domination. Furthermore, if for any reason the internal economy expanded to permit some integration of the middle sectors, the structure would be open to the risk of pressure by the popular classes for incorporation.

Prior to incorporation of the middle sectors, oligarchic groups of large landholders clearly predominated. Their economic support was the low-productivity latifundium with a preferably regional or internal market. The social relations of production followed the pattern of the traditional hacienda, as in Mexico, Venezuela, or Bolivia, and domination was exercised mainly over the peasant masses. The formal political game at the state level took place among oligarchic groups which, although competing with one another for better connections with the "outside," presented a solid front to the other social groups. In these conditions, the middle sectors necessarily limited their participation to attempts to break into the closed circle. For this purpose, they mobilized the peasant where the hacienda economy was the real base of internal power; they adopted a nationalist tone where the oligarchy appeared more clearly as intermediary for the enclave; and they mobilized additional, non-peasant, sectors where the enclave was mining.

Other historical situations arose in countries under enclave predominance when domination was not purely oligarchic but also included in various degrees the presence of bourgeois sectors. These groups maintained their economic and political positions vis-à-vis the enclave through a policy of retrenchment. The bourgeoisie could gain strength as an economic class not only by taking advantage of development possibilities in the mercantile and financial sectors, chiefly in the mining enclaves, as in the case of Chile, but also—with difficulty—through control of some agricultural sectors permitting a more capitalist exploitation of land, as in the case of the plantation owners along the Peruvian coast. In these conditions, development of the domestic economy made for a more complex social division of labor and for urban growth. While the middle sectors became more numerous, the presence of new urban popular sectors was added to the workers and peasants of enclave and hacienda.

The state also represented this greater complexity; it was the culmination of the power based on the hacienda, and it constituted a bureaucracy through which the interests of the oligarchic and bourgeois groups were expressed, subject to the constraints of their relations with the enclave. The state redistributed the taxes collected from the enclave economy and promoted internal economic activities. The most important sectors of the "middle class" were part of the state machinery.

In their efforts at incorporation, the middle sectors were faced with a system of domination that was structured principally through the relations of the oligarchic and bourgeois sectors with the enclave. They found that the dominated groups—the peasants of the hacienda or plantation, the workers of the agricultural or mining enclave, and the urban popular sectors—could be mobilized for a policy of collaboration. The political alternatives covered a broad spectrum of alliances that ranged from the possibility of taking advantage of a struggle within the dominant sector to become incorporated as the ally of one of the groups, as happened in Chile, to a revolutionary movement on the part of peasant and worker sectors, as was attempted by the Peruvian APRA (Alianza Popular Revolucionaria Americana).

Landholding groups could transform their type of economic activity into a form of agricultural exploitation that broke with the hacienda system without necessarily creating an urban-industrial economy. In this situation, peasants who were not incorporated into the enclave or the national capitalist agricultural exploitation were driven into forms of subsistence economy, as was the result of capitalist agricultural expansion in Central America. The limited advancement of social division of labor restricted the size of middle-class sectors. They could be incorporated into political life only insofar as the enclave and export economy created a service sector large enough to accommodate them; otherwise, they might try to mobilize the peasants against the system of domination. The alternative to this situation was gradual transformation of national agriculture to permit land distribution and, thereby, the emergence of middle and small landholders, as had occurred to some extent in Costa Rica.

INCORPORATION OF THE MIDDLE CLASS THROUGH A BREAKDOWN IN THE OLIGARCHIC DOMINATION: MEXICO, BOLIVIA, AND VENEZUELA

In some countries, the oligarchic domination was based on a mining enclave and on very traditional relations. In the rural areas of these countries, the middle class could effectively participate in the exercise of power only by enlisting support of the peasant and popular masses in order to carry out a revolution. This happened in Mexico and Bolivia and, to a lesser degree, in Venezuela. The peasant sectors played different roles in the revolutionary movements of the first two of these countries.

During the "Porfiriato" (1876–1911), Mexico recovered much of its economic dynamism thanks chiefly to renewed exploitation of its silver wealth located mainly in the north— Baja California, Chihuahua, and Durango. Copper mining was also developed in the El Boleo mines owned by the French and the Cananea mines owned by the United States. British and United States companies began to exploit petroleum in the Gulf of Mexico and to distribute it as crude oil. In 1910 three-quarters of the mines belonged to foreigners, and the mining law in effect since 1884 granted ownership of subsoil resources to the property owners. Together with the expansion of mining, there was some industrial development: lead and copper foundries, an iron and steel plant in Monterrey, cotton and woolen textile factories, food products, and so forth. Nevertheless, the industrial sector could not meet domestic demand; and trade was largely controlled by the United States, which also had invested heavily in the Mexican railway system. The Díaz policy was to play the interests of British, French, and United States capital against each other, but United States penetration had advanced so far that it was difficult to resist.

The agricultural process had special characteristics. The Reform laws continued to be applied for the purpose of land appropriation, and to this was added the action of the so-called surveying companies that operated under a colonization law promulgated in 1876. These companies were supposed to survey idle land and bring in foreign colonists to work it; their expenses were to be defrayed by transferring to the companies one-third of the surveyed land. The rest was sold cheaply to politicians and foreign speculators. It is estimated that between 1881 and 1889 land acquired without payment—the third transferred to the companies—and sold at giveaway prices reached 27,500,000 hectares, or more than 13 percent of the total area of the republic. Moreover, property concentration was enormous: one member of a surveying company acquired 7,000,000 hectares in Chihuahua; another, 2,000,000 in Oaxaca; two members, 2,000,000 in Durango, and four members, 11,500,000 in Baja California. In this way, eight individuals became owners of 22,500,000 hectares.[10]

When there was no more unused land to survey, the Indians were despoiled of their communal lands on the grounds that their property titles were not clear, and they were thus forced into peonage.

In spite of land appropriation, the agricultural economy continued to function. There were still many low-productivity latifundia, especially those growing cereals (at that time, Mexico had to import wheat and corn), whereas other agrarian sectors like sugar, coffee, sisal, and tobacco plantations as well as cattle ranches were modernized and even began to export.

Furthermore, the process of urbanization began to affect the northern states, which were the principal centers of production, and the combined population of cities of more than 20,000 inhabitants increased 44 percent from 1895 to 1910.

10. Jesús Silva Herzog, *Breve historia de la revolución mexicana* (Mexico: Fondo de Cultura Economica, 1960), pp. 16–17.

The middle sectors not linked to the production process and with little possibility of access to the higher government posts had also grown significantly, as is suggested by the fact that in 1910 Mexican schools had 900,000 students although the country's rate of illiteracy was 75 percent, which constituted progress in comparison with previous decades.

Despite its heavy dependence on the exterior, the economy of the Porfiriato managed to produce a diversification that was expressed in the social structure, which combined features of backwardness and development.[11] Although the Porfiriato state had served as a channel of ascent for many groups, it excluded others from political power. The old hacienda remained the most effective means of keeping the peasants submissive, and because Díaz needed its support, he could not open political power to the new groups even though they had been formed under his government. These same groups were also limited in their capacity of expression by his need to maintain an oligarchy.

If the new bourgeois groups and some of the middle sectors wanted to have representation in the Porfiriato system, they had to install an electoral system that would not be controlled exclusively by the government. The slogan that Díaz himself had used at the beginning of his career was now used against him: "No re-election and effective suffrage." The rigidity of the Porfirista regime left no alternative but a revolutionary movement in which the new groups had to enlist the peasants as allies in order to use them as an "army" against the repressive apparatus of the oligarchy.

The revolution unleashed forces that could not have been foreseen by those who began it. Against the dictatorship of Porfirio Díaz were aligned the peasant troops of Villa and

11. For an analysis of the social differentiation and its significance in the revolution, see Manuel Villa, *El surgimiento de sectores sociales medios y la revolución mexicana* (Santiago: FLAC-SO, 1970).

those of Zapata, whose vague aspirations were often in contradiction with the aspirations of the middle and bourgeois sectors. Also involved were the interests of foreign capitalists, especially of the United States. The allies in the revolution began to turn against each other. Madero, elected president in 1911, had to confront Zapata and his peasants of the south who had proposed the Plan of Ayala to give a more revolutionary content to Madero's agrarian program. The latter had only provided for restitution of illegally seized land. General Huerta, in league with former Porfiristas and with the complicity of the United States ambassador, assassinated Madero in 1913 and imposed his dictatorship. He was opposed by Zapata, Villa, and the farmers of Sonora led by General Obregón.

United States policy favored another anti-Porfirist leader, General Carranza, to whom Wilson delivered arms at the same time he ordered the landing of troops in Veracruz. After the downfall of Huerta, the conflict was now between Villa and Zapata allied against Carranza and Obregón, now in alliance. The latter mobilized peasant and worker support for Carranza; and the workers, who had not been very important in earlier battles, made up the "red battalions." Villa and Zapata were defeated and Carranza became president.

A new constitution was drafted in 1917 restoring the principle that land, water, and subsoil belonged to the nation. Ejido property was declared inalienable, and the worker was given the right to organize and to strike. But almost all of this remained on paper. The agrarian reform distributed only 18,000 hectares; there was repression; Zapata was assassinated in 1919; and the labor center "Casa del Obrero Mundial" was closed and its directors were imprisoned or murdered. Carranza began to have problems with the United States over petroleum. In 1920 Obregón and Calles took arms against Carranza, and when the latter tried to flee, he was ambushed and shot. Obregón was elected president in 1920, Calles in 1924, and Obregón again in 1928, only to be assassinated. Over the next six years there was a succession of presidents who were docile instruments of Calles. The system was supported by the peasant beneficiaries of the agrarian reform, the nationwide government-subsidized labor union known as CROM, and the party founded by Calles, which, after a series of names, was finally called the Partido Revolucionario Institucional (PRI).

The revolution had not done away completely with the links of dependence on foreign capital. As peasant and worker demands increased so did the instability of the regime. President Cárdenas ushered in a change with his government. His alliance with the popular sectors signified agrarian reform, more ejidos (common land controlled by peasant communities), and the organization of a strong union apparatus to replace the previous one that had become corrupt. Furthermore, he launched a vigorous nationalization program with the ultimate objective of nationalizing petroleum. With these measures he secured effective popular support for the regime. The scheme was unusual in that while it reinforced the power of the state, it also established a private form of economic power parallel to that of the state.

In the case of Bolivia,[12] the oligarchy began to break down politically with the fiasco of the Chaco War. For the first time after the war, the Indian was taken into account in terms of power, and there was even some possibility of incorporating him into the nation. Furthermore, the middle sectors—composed of young officers of the Chaco War, university intellectuals, and a few small political groups—were dissatisfied with the oligarchic domination and sought somehow to replace it. These groups found an effective ally in the tin miners, which resulted in the Movimiento Nacionalista Revolucionario (National Revolutionary Movement). It should

12. For a good summary of the Bolivian revolution and its social background, see the article by Richard W. Patch, "Bolivia: U.S. Assistance in a Revolutionary Setting," in R. N. Adams, O. Lewis, et al., *Social Changes in Latin America Today* (New York: Harper & Brothers, 1960), pp. 108ff.

be noted that the peasant movement had been developing its own, more radical action since 1936 and was not at first incorporated into the MNR.

Under the wartime government of Peñaranda, tin—the basis of the export economy—was sent to the United States for smelting, and petroleum concessions were granted in the same way. This spurred the urban anti-oligarchic movement, which was nationalist with fascist overtones. Worker pressures also intensified, and strikes in 1942 were savagely repressed. An army coup, acting in alliance with the majority party MNR, installed Major Villarroel as president in 1944. The Trotskyite party, Partido Obrero Revolucionario, now entered the political game. Mine owners and their foreign associates blocked the reformist attempts of the Villarroel government, which found itself unable to fulfill the economic and social promises it had made to its worker allies. The overthrow of the Villarroel government temporarily ended the threat to oligarchic dominance.

After the frustrated attempt to open the structure of domination through the military-popular alliance represented by the Villarroel government (1944–1946), the middle class and the tin miners, this time in conjunction with the urban-popular masses of the capital, tried again to displace the oligarchic and enclaves system. Subsequent policy therefore called for nationalization of mines. It might thus appear that urban-mining radicalism was not concerned with the agrarian sector.[13] Nevertheless, the dynamic of the peasant movement obliged the middle class to add agrarian reform to its political program. Even though the peasant groups did not actively engage in the game of power, they became an important area of support for the urban-popular policies of the middle classes after the Revolution of 1953 and the rise of Paz Estenssoro.

13. For a study of the relations between agrarian reform and revolution in Bolivia, see Flavio Machicado Saravia, *Ensayo crítico sobre la reforma agraria: una interpretación teórica del caso boliviano* (mimeographed dissertation for the Department of Economics, University of Chile, Santiago, 1966).

In Venezuela, the struggle between the various regional oligarchies culminated in a military regime which, although it did not affect the local power of the oligarchies, did not permit them to continue to fight for supremacy among themselves either.

The pact with the petroleum companies, which was concluded during the military regime, altered the traditional Venezuelan situation. Development of the urban sector permitted formation of a substantial middle class, and the petroleum enclave gave rise to the first large concentrations of workers.

The middle class organized an opposition to the regime based on the urban middle sectors and the petroleum workers. It was unlikely that this alliance could in itself constitute a real threat to the prevailing system. Since there was no possibility of holding an election, the only alternative was violent action. Even this was difficult because the middle class was urban and its allies, the petroleum workers of the Gulf of Maracaibo, were distant from these centers. Furthermore, the support of the urban popular sectors diminished to the degree that petroleum generated profits to be redistributed by the state in Caracas.

The only alternative left to the middle sectors consisted in taking advantage of conflicts in the power structure, specifically among the military groups, in order to foment a coup. The military uprising of General Medina Angarita, which was supported on condition that he restore democratic procedures, was the result of that alternative. With the way opened to election, the Partido Acción Democrática (Party of Democratic Action), which expressed the alliance between middle class and petroleum workers, took over the government with Rómulo Betancourt in 1945 and instituted the first measures to alter the base of traditional power. A land reform was undertaken and better terms were wrested from the petroleum enclave. In 1947, Rómulo Gallegos of Acción Democrática was elected president of the republic. Nonetheless, the power of Acción Democrática was ephemeral; one of the important elements in the overthrow of the previous regime, the military, turned against this government party in 1948 and set up an authoritarian government with Pérez Jiménez (1952–1958), supported by the profits from its relation with the enclave.

The period of Pérez Jiménez coincided with a boom in petroleum exports, which accelerated the growth of Caracas. External capitalism not only invested in petroleum, but it also made heavy investments in commercial and industrial activities for the domestic market. These activities engendered popular sectors that no longer depended solely on the state and were prepared to press their own claims. As the base of opposition broadened to include the middle sectors, urban-popular sectors and petroleum workers, an uprising became more viable, the more so because it could count on at least the tacit support of the peasants, who remembered the land reform program initiated by Acción Democrática during its brief administration. After Pérez Jiménez was ousted in 1958, Acción Democrática returned to power; but on its modifying the orientation of foreign investment, now directed to more than just petroleum, some of the victorious middle groups clashed over their participation in the new activities and this led to a virtual breakdown of the earlier alliance.

ACCESS OF THE MIDDLE CLASS TO THE
OLIGARCHIC-BOURGEOIS DOMINATION

Success—In Chile, control of the state and therefore of the profits generated by the enclave was in the hands of the local oligarchy and of a mercantile-financial bourgeoisie. In addition to maintaining important economic sectors, this bourgeoisie acted as junior partner or, in some cases, as agent of the foreign enterprises that exploited the enclave sector. The growth of cities ushered in a middle class dedicated to the liberal professions or to public service. A proletariat was being formed that was directly tied to the nitrate enclave economy or to related activities such as ports and transport. Finally, there was an urban mass which, although it included a large number of craftsmen and did not yet constitute an industrial worker sector, to some extent added its demands to those of the above groups.

After 1884 the nitrate economy, now in the hands of British capital, continued to be the major source of revenue, and exports increased notably during the war. United States capital began to displace British capital at this time. A technological reason was that the Guggenheim system of nitrate exploitation made possible the use of lower-grade limestone than did the British Shanck system. United States banks supplanted the British Rothchilds as creditors of the state. After World War I, United States trade dominated the Chilean market. Nevertheless, although conditions for the change in foreign trade were favorable, the post-war years were a period of bond issues, inflation, and inconvertible paper currency. Speculation and negotiations with the state were everyday occurrences. The groups most affected by the domestic policies were the popular sectors, whose demands were met with repression—the massacre of the nitrate mine workers at Iquique, the murder of workers and the dissolution of the trade-union organization in Punta Arenas, and the violent repressions in Santiago and Valparaiso. With the end of World War I the situation became worse, for not only was nitrate less in demand but it was being replaced by synthetic nitrate. "Nitrate revenues fell 36 percent from 1918 to 1921 and 1922."[14]

The political scheme of power also was shattered in 1920. Although the dominant national groups shared power with the state, they never stopped fighting among themselves in addition to their conflicts with the popular sectors.

The slump following World War I affected the enclave economy and—through the connecting mechanisms of banks, domestic trade, and import-export trade—the economy as a whole. It became necessary to readjust the imbalance

14. Aníbal Pinto, *Chile, un caso de desarrollo frustrado* (Santiago: Editorial Universitaria, 1959), p. 63.

of power thus created. One possibility was to shift from the English scheme to closer ties with the United States, which now appeared to be the axis of the economy, and to do so required the incorporation of a new social sector into the system of power. The alliance was made with the urban middle class by incorporating it electorally. A new political balance was thereby established in terms of a legality that not only justified "ownership of part of the country" but also legitimized "ownership of the votes." In this alliance, known in the 1920s as *Alessandrismo,* the urban middle class, by joining the state, could share in the profits the latter derived from the enclave economy, which was not controlled mainly by United States capital. At first, the middle sectors did not question the advantages of an enclave economy. Their chief interest was not so much to create a new economic base that would give them a measure of autonomy or enable them to compete with existing national economic groups as it was to try to strengthen the state as the organization they administered.

Although the popular sectors were mobilized together with the middle class, they never considered the presence of the middle class in the state, voting rights, and so forth to be more than political gains, whereas their main battleground was the economy itself. Perhaps for this reason, while the popular sectors supported the new accord, they could never be counted on as permanent, reliable allies. The economic system with its ups and downs could not be reconciled with the interests of the popular masses through political programs alone, and this led to severe conflicts among the ruling classes as well as to friction between these and the popular sectors.

In their contest for control of the state, the various groups would often turn to a strong-man regime as a last resort. Initially, it was the new middle sectors that had pressed for a stronger executive.

The crisis in the enclave economy upset the balance that had been introduced by the presence of the middle classes. The first government of Alessandri was overthrown in 1924 by a military junta whose members (Altamirano, Nell, and Benett) could not attempt a simple restoration even though they had been involved in the displaced British scheme. Especially through its commanding officers the army represented large sectors of the middle class that were to wield great influence. This was typified by Colonel Carlos Ibáñez. Return to oligarchic dominance was not possible, but the struggle among the factions of the middle sectors and the bourgeois group, whose alliances and conflicts were expressed in the leadership of Alessandri and Ibáñez, prevented stability. The one point of agreement was the need to develop more and closer ties with the United States.

Because no attempt had been made to create a new economic structure, the system lacked the dynamism needed to cope with unemployment. Stopgap measures like public works and other activities were promoted, but such policies failed because they represented enormous expenditures and indebtedness that were not acceptable to either the bourgeoisie or the local oligarchy. As economic measures, they did little to still the unrest of the jobless masses or of those threatened by loss of employment.

Political action was generally directed toward the repression of both the radicalized urban middle class (students) and organized labor. There was no support for governments that tried in desperation to solve their difficulties by reestablishing alliances with the local oligarchies. These struggles even made possible a short-lived socialist republic, which lasted twelve days. Conflict between the various social groups was serious; Rightist and Leftist violence and armed militia became more than theoretical possibilities.

The most practicable way to confront the crisis was to reconstruct the political alliance of the traditional sectors by incorporating a few sectors of the urban middle class, especially the least radicalized, as was the case in the second government of Arturo Alessandri in 1932. Subsequent economic policies were somewhat more progressive, although certainly not populist in character. Inflation was used as a way of furnishing credits to the national agricultural and industrial groups; however, it was not offset by an increase in real wages for the workers.

As the urban middle class began to recover from the effects of the Great Depression, it could again think in terms of joining the power structure of the state. With the easing of the economic crisis, the popular sectors also could make common cause with the "political programs" of sectors of the middle class and accept a policy of redistribution. Furthermore—and this was to some degree a by-product of their earlier battles—they were now sufficiently organized to be considered allies and not just a mass of workers. Their participation was expressed in the Popular Front of 1938.

The urban middle class reentered government administration with a new purpose: to create for itself an economic power base by using the state to promote an industrial economy which it would manage and which would enable it to associate with the mercantile-financial bourgeoisie, not just as an electoral force but also as an emerging bourgeoisie in its own right.

Failure—In Peru, the conservative government of Balta introduced its export scheme through agreements entered into by the minister of finance, Nicolas Piérola, who came from the Arequipa aristocracy. In 1869, Piérola gave the Dreyfus Company a monopoly of guano exports, thereby breaking with the system of concessions traditionally granted to local merchants for the exploitation of guano. With this, the aristocracy of Lima, composed basically of merchants and owners of coastal sugar and cotton plantations, temporarily yielded their advantage to foreign interests. The guano concession was followed by a railway program favoring the British and by loans to the government. These loans were secured by future sales of guano and were used to finance public expenditures and to redistribute the government income from foreign exploitation to the dominant local groups. Not only was railway investment promoted under the management of the United States immigrant Henry Meiggs, later associated with financial institutions of the United States, England, and France, but the exploitation of Peru's mineral and agricultural resources was intensified by companies like Grace and Gildemeister. The redistribution policy and corruption in the state created a swelling sector of speculators, bureaucrats, white-collar workers, and military men.

The reaction to this policy was the *civilista* movement headed by Manuel Pardo, who became president in 1872. The world economic crisis of the following year created difficulties for the civilista government.

Manuel Pardo was succeeded by General Prado, whose government presided over expansion of the nitrate industry and then entered the War of the Pacific with Chile in 1879 over control of nitrate deposits. Peru emerged from the war impoverished and more than ever dominated by the British. The Dreyfus Company was supplanted by a British firm, and control of nitrate also passed into the hands of British or Chilean intermediaries. Railways, ports, and customs met the same fate. There was a period of military *caudillismo,* until Piérola himself, who had been opposed by *civilismo,* drove the military from power in 1895 after a bloody civil war.

Piérola was now a caudillo with broad support from the urban popular sector of Lima, thanks to his triumph over militarism. When he returned to power, he modernized the state; that is, he prepared it for a new form of insertion of the export economy into the international market through the enclave controlled by the British. The prevailing political system, in spite of its form as a liberal-representative model, primarily benefited the plantation owners on the coast, the merchants in Lima, and the landholders of the sierra. The British-controlled enclave permitted national producers and intermediaries to share in the income from the exploitation of natural resources and local workers imposed as much by nationals as by foreigners.

After the 1873 slump and the disaster of the War of the Pacific, the expansion of new sectors of the export economy was based on the development of the enclave economy. From the beginning of the twentieth century the presence of the United States began to be felt. Copper, having risen from next to nothing in 1857 to 10,000 tons (worth about a half-million pounds) in six years time,[15] was taken over by the United States and operated as a modern production unit. Although national entrepreneurial interests, which had been accustomed to the old-style British capitalism and had their political expression in the *civilismo* party, tried to compel the United States entrepreneurs to associate with them, both copper and sugar were increasingly controlled by large foreign companies. The sugar mill oppressed the sugar planter, and the large mining interests destroyed the small mineowner. Local entrepreneurs, usually in a position marginal to the market or subordinate to foreigners, shifted to banking, services, and industry. Most of these activities centered in Lima, which in 1903 was the only city of some importance, with 319,409 inhabitants and 259 foreign residents in the capital together with its port at Callao.

Politically, but in a form different from that of the Balta-Piérola period of 1869, the new Piérola government incorporated the old mercantile and financial sectors of Lima into the alliance with the enclave sector. Although this political model did not open the way to more participation of the middle classes, it did have some success with the urban masses now increased through expansion of the enclave export economy.

Economically, the *civilismo* policy of the twentieth century was characterized by adoption of the gold standard, economic liberalism, and strict adherence to export interests. The mining code was changed to permit private appropriation; the administrative machinery was rationalized to serve the interests of mining export; and commercial and banking laws were reformed. In short, the economy was integrated into the new model of the export enclave.

The dynamism of the export economy withstood the consequences of the opening of the Panama Canal in 1914

15. These and subsequent data are taken from E. Yepes del Castillo, *Peru 1820–1920: un siglo de desarrollo capitalista* (Lima: Instituto de Estudios Peruanos, Campodónico Ediciones, 1972).

and of the World War of 1914–1918. The market for copper was in the United States, for sugar, in South America, and there was a growing market for cotton. The United States penetrated still further into the Peruvian economy: its investments rose from 6 million dollars in 1897 to 63 million dollars in 1914. Between 1913 and 1917 United States investment doubled from 30 to 60 million dollars, while British investment fell from 33 to 18 million dollars.

This expansion entailed expropriation of the lands of small farmers, especially along the coast, for extension of the enclaves; disintegration of the subsistence economy with the introduction of capitalism; and centralization of economic activities in Lima. The result was urbanization without industrialization; immigration; and rural and urban poverty coexisting with export prosperity. The Indian economy of the high sierra remained untouched except in the mining areas, where an identical process of expropriation and proletarianization took place. The system of *enganche* and other forms of forced labor ensured the base of capitalist-export exploitation in Peru, and repression of workers completed the ingredients for ''progress.''

It was the very dynamism of the enclave economy with its social consequences, the impoverishment of the masses and the concommitant rural and urban proletarianization, that laid the foundation for the protest of the masses. Unlike the socio-political process of countries where the enclave economy was formed in the preceding century, in Peru the pressure of the masses arose before the political system was opened to the middle sectors. The rise in basic food prices, the lengthening of the workday, and so forth generated strikes, especially after 1905, not only in Lima and Callao (for example, on March 1, 1908) but also in the sugar plantations and mining zones (strikes by the workers of the Cerro de Pasco Railway in 1909, of the Chiclayo Valley in 1910, etc.).

This was the background of the attempts by Leguía in his first government of 1912 to turn *civilista* democracy into ''authoritarian progressiveness.'' Because of the ensuing split in *civilismo,* the orthodox followers of Leguía could not impose their candidate, and Billinghurst, the Arequipa merchant who had made a fortune in nitrate, became president. His brief government showed that in the Peruvian political model it was impossible to reconcile the pressure of the masses, which had brought him to power and which remained strong (there was a general strike of workers in Lima in 1913), with the permanent interests of the dominant system.

The army from the interior, led by General Benavides, deposed the president in 1914, revealing the weakness of the *civilista* political model in the new conditions. The interregnum of the second government of José Pardo from 1915 to 1919 could not prevent social pressures, strikes, and repressions. The dictatorship of Leguía from 1919 to 1930 represented the new authoritarian and "developmentalist" model in its support of the United States enclave. Nonetheless, as though the Balta government had been revived in new conditions, Leguía weakened the position of the Lima oligarchy by incorporating new sectors of the national dominant groups through his program of public works, urban expenditures, and expanded bureaucracy.

The Lima oligarchy again resorted to the army in order to reestablish its influence. First it was Sánchez Cerro who toppled Leguía and with *civilista* support was elected president in 1932. After the assassination of Sánchez Cerro, Benavides governed the country as a direct representative of the oligarchy until 1939, when Manuel Prado was chosen to be president in elections managed by Benevides.

The transition period of Peru had begun with Billinghurst or, more precisely, with Leguía. This period must be understood in terms of not only the pressure of popular forces but also the ideology with which the middle classes confronted the political situation. The content of southern South American radicalism and of Brazilian *tenentismo** was uni-

*Translator's note: rebellion of young officers against coffee oligarchy and its allies.

versal suffrage and free elections. This implied a social up-
heaval in the Peruvian situation. The pressure of the social
situation drove Peruvian intellectuals to a more profound examination of the political process. Mariátegui, ideologist and
communist leader, exemplified this approach. His discussion
of the isolation of the Indians in the sierra and their exploitation in a country where they made up two-thirds of the
population, as well as of the nascent proletariat, led to more
radical criticism. It was no longer possible to accept the economic export scheme and ask only for participation in a
broader democracy. Although the APRA (Alianza Popular
Revolucionaria Americana) party of Haya de la Torre was an
alliance between sectors of the middle classes, the urban
proletariat, and the wage-earning farm workers, from the
early 1930s it had a political content that went beyond the
radicalism of the middle class without aiming for a purely
populist incorporation of the masses into the bourgeois-
oligarchic state.

During this period, strong-man regimes were a permanent fixture in Peruvian life, in part because of the fierce
infighting among the ruling sectors. The middle class was
caught between allying itself as a junior partner with the
bourgeoisie that had adopted the more modern urban or
agrarian forms of capitalism and joining forces with the popular sectors.

The APRA was the party with a program that most
approximated the possibility of a populist movement directed by the middle class, but there were obviously other alternatives, such as the paternalistic populism attempted on
different occasions and in varying circumstances by Piérola,
Leguía, and Sánchez Cerro.

The many possibilities of alliance produced by the
numerous conflicts created a weak point in the system of
dominance. Attempts to exploit this weakness, such as the
sometimes violent efforts of the APRA party to shatter the
system (as in the Trujillo uprising of 1934) were brutally repressed. As a result, the APRA was for some time prohibited

from participating in the electoral process. This explains the
appearance of regimes controlled by the military, which not
only covered up the oligarchic-bourgeois domination but also
served to contain popular pressures.

The middle sectors lost strength. Even their alliance with
the popular sectors was weakened, for they began to abandon
popular support in order to seek power through coalitions
with the ruling modern or more traditional groups. They
believed that they could use the cracks in the state apparatus
to gain a position of advantage from which they could then
entrench themselves by means of a broader alliance. However,
such complicated tactics only hampered their project because
the dominant groups were wary of an ally who might conceal
the presence of the popular sectors that could threaten the
established scheme of domination. The dominant groups
preferred to maintain a form of power that ensured continuance of the prevailing system. Later, the alliances changed
in content and direction, when some of the more progressive
mercantile-financial sectors tried to recover the support of
the masses, as occurred during the early days of *Belaundismo.*
The middle class, especially the *Apristas,* chose to risk losing
part of their popular support by seeking allies like the *Odri-
ístas* who were better situated within the system of traditional
power.

THE MIDDLE CLASS VIS-À-VIS THE LANDHOLDERS
AND THE ENCLAVE

In Central America, considered as a whole, the transformation of the "agrarian oligarchy" into "agrarian capitalists
exporting groups" eliminated the hacienda as a production
system, but did not generate significant urban-industrial activity. Although a detailed discussion of national historical
processes might modify the analysis, for purposes of this
study our approach to certain topics can be applied to the
area as a whole.

After Independence, the Central American export economy continued to depend on some colonial products, especially animal and vegetable dyes, while agricultural and

livestock activities were still important in domestic output. The social structure reflected the economy; merchants connected with dye export wielded decisive influence because of their control over loans to farmers, who were generally *minifundistas,* that is to say, very small proprietors.

But not all was dye: there were also hacienda-type estates, extensive communal lands, and large tracts of ecclesiastic properties or land in mortmain. This situation changed with the coffee cycle that began about 1870. The "Liberal regime," which paralleled the coffee boom, instituted the process of land appropriation. Communal land, land in mortmain, and even many minifundia were converted into private holdings—actually into property of large landholders who enthusiastically embarked on the new agriculture. During this cycle, the coffee growers managed to displace the merchant moneylenders by creating their own credit system, chiefly through domestic banks. This marked the beginning of such infrastructure works as railroads.

The formation of the banana enclave in the hands of United States capital coincided with the expansionist policy of that country, which even employed military intervention in Central America and the Caribbean. The banana companies exercised a virtual monopoly over the railroads and fruit-loading ports. Although banana exports did not often exceed coffee exports, this change took place when the price of coffee declined in the world market. The importance of the banana enclave was based on its having added transport to its domain.

The 1929 depression was felt in Central America in reduced exports, and although the peasants could take refuge in a subsistence economy, recovery began only toward the end of the 1940s. The depression revealed the character of the domination. In El Salvador, where a rebellion of starving peasants had been put down with the execution of thirty thousand of the insurgents, it became clear that the system was based on the ability of a sector—the landholder in combination with the enclave interests—to hold in fief the peasant population as a source of cheap labor, making possible high profits. The succession of strong-man regimes at this time proved that even in adverse conditions there was an effort to keep the situation unchanged.

The urban middle class, which grew relatively slowly in Central America, also suffered repression. Their demands for political participation could therefore lead indirectly to peasant uprisings. As the oligarchy preferred to maintain the status quo, the middle sectors were left with two alternatives: to accept control by the sectors tied to the authoritarian oligarchy and enclave, which would condemn the peasant to continued subjugation; or to embark on a campaign of political pressure that might get out of hand.

An example of the foregoing was the Guatemalan revolution, from the time Arévalo came to power in 1944 until the fall of Arbenz in 1954. Land reform set off a strong reaction, and the government that succeeded Arbenz tried to turn back to the previous situation. The middle class could only begin to participate when, during recent years, sectors connected with government circles began to modernize the agricultural economy—chiefly cotton plantations—that developed because of the need to increase exports; and they incorporated a level of technology that was no longer predominantly labor intensive. This permitted growth of cities and urban functions that, although linked to agricultural exploitation, were not so dependent on the maintenance of huge contingents of peasants. On the other hand, there was little industrialization and consequently little possibility of popular pressure channeled through often short-lived labor unions.

MIDDLE CLASS, INDUSTRIALIZATION, AND POLITICS

Because of the weakness of their bourgeois sector, countries dominated by an enclave economy had a rudimentary domestic market. Within the range of possible variants in this type of economy, there were only two cases of policies concerned with expansion of such a market, that is, with industrialization. The first case included countries like Chile where the external sector imposed itself when there already existed an important mercantile-financial sector and therefore a middle class capable of creating the national bases for economic expansion. The second case included countries like Mexico and Venezuela where by revolution the middle sectors entered the state apparatus and used it to create a national economy. In all cases, the domestic economy developed through pressure from the middle groups allied with the existing bourgeois capitalist sector, or with the worker-peasant sector, or with both.

On the other hand, it should be pointed out that, although the Great Depression directly and adversely affected the modern sector—that is, the enclave—in those countries, it did not threaten the dominance of the oligarchic groups, because it did not touch the latter's economic foundation, which was the hacienda. Nevertheless, the enclave recession could not be offset, as occurred in countries with national producers, by policies to maintain the level of employment and by domestic investment. On the contrary, because of the unemployment produced by the depression, political confrontations took place in still more rigid social conditions. The 1930s were characterized by increased social pressure, numerous strikes, and more radical policies: *Cardenismo* in Mexico; the radical-socialist-communist "Popular Front" in Chile; *Aprismo* during its most revolutionary phase (the Trujillo uprising); the founding of the Venezuelan Democratic Action party; the peasant insurgency in El Salvador; the incorporation of many peasants into the armed rebellion of Sandino; and, finally, the "socializing" attempts in Bolivia and Ecuador.

The response to popular pressure, which was directed by segments of the middle class, was armed force on the part of the dominant oligarchy and enclave. In these conditions, creating a domestic market required previous policy to be changed, as it was in Chile, Mexico, Venezuela, and, later, in Peru. The economic consequences of the "transition"— that is, the rise of the middle classes or, in some cases, the transformation of the most privileged strata of these classes into a nascent bourgeoisie—did not derive from the world economic crisis, as it did in countries with a national export economy. Only a breakdown or at least a recession in the sector linked to the oligarchy and to the enclave would make it possible to use the state, already partly controlled by other groups, to bring about the investment needed to form a domestic market, which in turn would support a new policy.

In the subsequent history of these countries, developmentalist populism no longer had support, and the formation of an industrializing bourgeoisie depended, by and large, on the state. Moreover, with state participation and with public-sector financing derived increasingly from income generated by the enclave sectors, the rising middle class and the recently constituted or (as in Chile and to a lesser extent in Peru) the longer-established national bourgeoisie tried to change the patterns of development by strengthening the urban-industrial sector. With the exception of Chile, this was what happened after World War II in the countries dominated by an enclave economy. The links of external dependence were of another kind, as will be seen in the discussion that follows. From 1950 on, foreign investments would be made in the production sector oriented to the domestic market, and this would set new limitations and open new possibilities for national development.

CHAPTER FIVE

Nationalism and Populism

Social and Political Forces of Development in the Phase of Consolidating the Domestic Market

The distinctive feature of the transition period in Latin America in the relations among social groups and classes was the growing participation of the urban middle classes and of the industrial and commercial bourgeoisie in the system of domination.

The social situation was expressed on an economic level by policies to consolidate the domestic market and to industrialize. In countries where the export economy was controlled by national groups that had succeeded in forming an important industrial sector *before* the foreign trade crisis, these policies took on a more liberal cast. That is, they were based on the expansion of private enterprise. In countries where exports were controlled mainly by an enclave, groups not tied directly to the import-export system had tried to create an urban-industrial base through state direction. In some countries the state apparatus had been used as an instrument in the formation of an industrial class, which eventually would share entrepreneurial functions with the state-owned enterprises.

The private sector was not excluded from economies where state participation was preponderant, nor was the public sector absent in the initial stage of industrialization, even in countries of liberal tradition. On the contrary, the import-substitution phase of industrialization was characterized by two converging movements: growth of the private sector of the economy, and the creation of new areas of investment concentrated around basic industry and infrastructure works with heavy state participation.

Both of these new economic bases of development required broad changes in the social division of work. Countries that began to grow in these ways underwent a demographic-ecological transformation as a proletariat emerged and as a non-wage-earning popular sector developed in the cities. The growth rate of the latter sector usually was higher than the rate at which new jobs were generated by industrialization. This brought about the formation in Latin America of what came to be called "mass urban societies" in insufficiently industrialized economies.

The presence of masses, together with the beginnings of industry that produced more than just nondurable consumer goods, characterized the initial period of inward development. This period intensified during World War II and reached its peak in the 1950s. During this period, industrialization was "substitutive": it was made possible mainly by difficulties of importation and subsequently by lack of foreign exchange. It used and expanded the production base of the preceding period to meet domestic demand for consumer and intermediate goods.[1] In the process, the role of the state increased and changed in character. The state had fundamentally expressed the interests of exporters and landholders and had acted as agent for foreign investment. Now it intervened to set up protective tariffs, to transfer income from the export to the domestic sector, and to create the infrastructure needed to support the import-substitution industry. This was the time of national steel foundries, oil refineries, and electrical power stations.

These measures were taken in some countries only because they were the result of power alliances made during the transition period. Consequently, the industrialization achieved in these cases was not, at the beginning, the result of the gradual or revolutionary ascent of a typical industrial bourgeoisie.

More precisely, this industrialization was the result of a policy, agreed upon by the various sectors, that reconciled the development needs of a type of economy that not only created an economic base for the new groups (later to share power in the transition period) but also offered opportunities of socio-economic incorporation to the popular groups which because of their number and presence in the cities might otherwise alter the system of domination. The system of domination comprised the ascendant middle classes, the urban bourgeoisie, and sectors of the old export-import system, even including the owners of low-productivity latifundia.

During "substitutive" industrialization the agro-exporting and financial sectors as well as the urban middle and

1. Maria de Conceição Tavares, "Auge y declinación del proceso de sustitución de importaciones en el Brasil," *Boletín Económico de América Latina*, 9, no. 1 (1964).

industrial sectors shared and disputed control of the state. Appearing in some cases as the object of domination and in others as the supporting base were the popular sectors made up of their three typical components: the working class, the urban popular mass, and the peasant mass.

The different agreements reached in the various countries by the social forces meant that each country would have its own set of substitutive industrialization policies even when different countries shared the same economic or socio-political problems. These differences were largely related to the ways in which economies and national societies had been formed. The functions of the state and the characteristics of the entrepreneurial groups varied in the transition period according to whether or not the original situation had been one of the enclave. Later on, when the presence of masses became important in determining the forms of domination, there would also be differentiation in terms of the particularities of the popular sector of each country.

The masses were generally oriented toward participation and social and economic distributivism. The new dominant sectors generally favored continued national economic expansion, now directed to the domestic market. Their trend to nationalism made possible incorporation of the masses into the production system and, to varying degrees, into the political systems. The connection thus established gave meaning to "developmentalist populism." This ideology expressed conflicting interests: expanded consumption versus accelerated investment in heavy industries, state participation in development versus reinforcement of the private urban-industrial sector. An ideology like "developmentalist populism," in which contradictory goals could coexist, was an attempt to achieve a reasonable consensus and to legitimize the new power system based on an industrialization program offering benefits for all.

The creation of a domestic market required (1) availability of capital to be reinvested within the country; (2) availability of foreign exchange to finance industrialization;

(3) possibilities of income redistribution, even if limited, to permit some degree of incorporation of the masses; (4) public and private managerial ability to expand the domestic economy; (5) a minimum of efficiency and responsibility in state administration; (6) a political leadership capable of reconciling the conflicting interests of the different groups in the interest of the "nation."

Actually, since availability of capital and foreign exchange was in the hands of the exporting group, the above scheme could only be realized by mobilizing the industrial bourgeoisie, the state bureaucracy, and the worker-popular sectors against the interests of the former. The success of such a mobilization depended, on the one hand, on a favorable outlook for prices in the world market that would permit policies to maintain the value of exports while carrying out some form of exchange control. On the other hand, given the developmentalist alliance between the industrialist sectors and the worker-popular sectors, it also depended on tariff and monetary policies that would keep up the rate of industrial investment and simultaneously ensure at least an absolute increase in the number of individuals incorporated from the popular sectors into the industrial system, even if it failed to increase real wages and affected the agrarian sector and the traditional middle groups adversely. Thus the groups that tried to control the decision-making process to obtain a pattern of more distributivist development clashed with those that influenced public agencies to reorient price and fiscal policies toward capitalization of private and public enterprises.

History determined how these conditioning factors of industrialization combined, and how they then devised models of development. Nevertheless, by taking liberties with hallowed concepts we can speak of models of hierarchies of variables.

The distinctive features of industrialization policies in each country depended on how the roles of the state and of the industrial bourgeoisie were reconciled. The economic functions of the state were important, but so was the way in which the state, as an instrument of domination, expressed the interests of various groups.

The masses, already important in this period, were needed for the process of industrialization, as a labor-force but also as an integral part of the consumer market. They had to be taken into account by the groups in power to the extent that they ensured or rejected the latter's hegemony.

The industrial bourgeoisie, whether in an enclave economy or where production was controlled by national groups, typically appeared in the different countries in one of the following ways:

1. "Liberal" industrialization directed by private entrepreneurial sectors; this required the existence of a vigorous and hegemonic agro-exporting sector that was in some way also linked to the domestic market.

2. "National-populist" industrialization oriented politically by the drive of social forces like the bourgeoisie, the middle sectors, and the popular (trade union) sectors, and linked to the power apparatus. Together with the agro-exporting sector (even if in conflict with it), these forces shared to some extent the direction of the process of development.

3. Industrialization oriented by a "developmentalist state," a process in which the weakness of a domestic capitalist export-import sector was offset by a state program that through a tax system channeled investment and established the bases for an industrial economy. This case appeared more often in the enclave situation.

In all cases, the problem of industrialization consisted in knowing which groups could take investment and market decisions and channel investment into the domestic market. It was, moreover, extremely difficult to incorporate—popular as well as low middle class—socially by industrialization. This was why nationalism and populism together expressed the attempts by developing societies to harmonize the interests of groups that were opposed to each other but that united among themselves for the purpose of finding a new base for national power.

Countries to be considered in the following pages are preferably those in which the characteristics of industrialization were more striking or showed more clearly the various possible alternatives.

Populism and the Free Enterprise Economy

In Argentina, both the phases of outward development and the period of transition expressed the dynamism of a hegemonic entrepreneurial agro-exporting sector. The system of domination embraced groups that were differentiated at the regional level. Therefore, when the effects of the crisis in world markets began to be felt and World War II intensified the conditions favoring industrialization, an industrial bourgeoisie already existed. It was linked to the agro-exporting sector through the financial system. There was also a middle class that was part of the political game and was capable of mobilizing, at least electorally, the urban popular sectors. The unionized-worker sectors tried to obtain their own representation chiefly through their unions and in some cases in association with parties such as the socialist one, especially in large urban centers like Buenos Aires and Rosario.

The dynamism and success of the exporting sector permitted the creation of an industrial sector dependent on it, and also a strong financial importing sector. These were the groups that undertook to develop the economy by taking advantage of the favorable prospects for the domestic market derived from economic prospects after the depression and especially during World War II. Politically their problem was to keep control of the expanding economy and, at the same time, to contain the worker-union pressure represented by the guild associations dating from the turn of the century. To this was added the pressure of the radical *Irigoyenismo* of the middle classes. During this period in Argentina there were also efforts to form a popular front (1944–1945) similar to those established in Europe and in Chile. Although unsuccessful, such efforts highlighted the class content of the political confrontation between a dominant bourgeoisie and a worker opposition. Nor were they unrelated to a postwar reaction against segments of the Argentine Right that had been overtly sympathetic to the Axis cause.

Nevertheless, the continued class domination—which eventually excluded all opposition—together with the dynamism of the economy, led to a dead end. The new contingents that were constantly being mobilized and incorporated into the labor force required by economic expansion were not being incorporated politically. Nor were they represented in the old trade union structure, where their presence, although broadening the base of worker policy, would have endangered the economic advantages already achieved. This situation was to end in the breakdown of both the exclusive bourgeois domination and the union structure of the old sectors of the working class.[2]

Peronist populism tried to find a solution to such problems and to give continuity to economic growth by respecting the impetus of the private enterprise sector but setting a general course to accelerate incorporation of the masses not only economically but also socially and therefore politically. The state became arbitrator for the class struggle and was used as a mechanism for income distribution both within the entrepreneurial class and downward.

Conflicts among the various sectors—principally between the worker-popular mass and the bourgeoisie—were expressed mainly as a confrontation between popular sectors and oligarchy without any specific political content beyond an abstract anti-foreign sentiment on the international level and pressure for higher wages. Why then did this confrontation appear crucial to the political reorientation of Argentina?

The agro-exporting groups exercised their hegemony in alliance with rural sectors that were basically of two types:

2. For the characteristics of this process, see Gino Germani, *Política y sociedad en una época de transición: de la sociedad tradicional a la sociedad de masas* (Buenos Aires: Paidós, 1962); also Torcuato De Tella, *El sistema político argentino y la clase obrera* (Buenos Aires: Eudeba, 1964).

the latifundista groups not directly linked to the exporting sector, and the rural sectors allied with but subordinate to the exporting sector. In Argentina the former were residual because of their low level of investment in agriculture; but the second were significant. They included farmers producing for the domestic market, rural bourgeoisie not linked to the agro-exporting sector, those that raised but did not fatten beef cattle, and finally grain farmers not linked to the marketing groups. The hegemonic group itself was made up precisely of the local sectors tied to the import-export scheme, which was basically foreign and increasingly monopolistic.

The hegemonic group of the agro-exporting sector was, through its investments in the domestic market, dynamic and developmentalist; on the other hand, it was the nexus of dependence. The new power coalition represented by *Peronismo* would be effective if it could reconcile the accumulation interests of the economically dominant sector with the participation interests of the expanding masses. Thanks to the foreign exchange accumulated during World War II, it was possible to improve wages and social conditions of the worker-popular sector and of middle-class white-collar workers without doing too much damage to the economically hegemonic sector of the previous stage, although certainly affecting the latter's subordinate sectors, the estancieros and the traditional urban middle class. These sectors, which in political language would be called the "oligarchy," were increasingly to pay the cost of the new power combination as the favorable balance of the export economy was depleted. They also were to bear the brunt of the political criticism of a system of power that was accused of being reactionary and in which they had hardly participated.

Industrialization under *Peronismo* followed two complementary courses: on the one hand, the import-export and financial sectors tried to regulate the impulse of industrialization in a way that could slow down and limit the policy of import substitution, at least in those products that were of interest to the hegemonic sector in its importing phase; on the other hand, the industrial sector not linked to the agro-exporting group tried to strengthen its economic base by expanding the area of substitutive industrialization and creating its own financing mechanisms, traditionally a weak point in this group. The state was a vital institution for both sectors: for the first, because it still controlled the exchange and tariff systems, which were fundamental to a balanced policy of industrial and agro-exporting interests; and for the second, because the state also represented an important instrument of credit and rapid capital formation.

In this development model the various social forces did not exert sufficient pressure to transform the state from an instrument of economic regulation into one directly promoting production. The already existing former economic base permitted private sectors to diversify the domestic economy without the public sector becoming an indispensable part of the production system. To create an industrial economy, private accumulation required only the state to redistribute income into its own investment channels. The resulting growth would generate employment opportunities at the rate adequate to incorporate the urban mass into the economic system.

This development model was possible because the economy was dynamic enough to convert the agricultural worker into a wage earner and to expand rapidly enough to absorb a large part of the rural-urban migration. Migration was accompanied by strong socio-political pressures that, nonetheless, were not directed toward creating a state production base to control economic decisions. Even when pressure for redistribution led to direct economic action by the state, the result was to reinforce the private sector because of the corporative linkage between the bourgeoisie and the new state enterprises.

The presence of masses was felt as a pressure of those who wanted to enter the system as a new partner accepting the already established rules on how industrialization was to be carried out, but who still demanded certain rights. There was strong pressure for higher wages and recognition of the rights of workers. But this did not exclude the possibility of combining the interests of different groups in the new power coalition. The masses were mobilized principally through the unions, and more as an employed mass than as an oppressed class. Their mobilization symbolized the policy of confrontation and of pooled interests through which the popular sectors established their relations with the industrial bourgeoisie. Jointly, these two sectors no longer acted precisely as allies of the monopolistic agro-exporting group, but all three certainly participated in the same power game and together formed a power coalition. So fluid and complex a political connection was made possible by their agreement not to make economic claims for the state; private monopoly was not to be threatened by state monopoly. This arrangement was favored by the prosperity that followed on World War II and by the rapid process of import substitution, which not only expanded mass consumption and raised wages but also capitalized industrial enterprises without lowering the profits of the monopolies.

This development was limited by the progressive exhaustion of the economic process of rapid import-substitution of nondurable and durable consumer goods. It was also limited by the contradiction in giving the masses greater participation in the distribution of national revenues while accelerating capital formation and trying to maintain the incomes of other social groups and, especially, of the agro-exporting sectors.

With the end of the easy phase of import substitution and of populist support within the framework of a liberal economy, reciprocal connections were undone. Simple theories began to give way to polemics over statism versus big business. This issue was to be the crossroads of development. The earlier schemes of political support fell apart, and the apparent polarization of oligarchy and popular sectors that had been cloaked by the "developmentalist alliance" was replaced by a new type of confrontation where certain class values served to catalyze popular behavior and, at the same time, to weaken national emphasis on the activities of the entrepreneurial groups. The latter proceeded to reorganize themselves, and tried to reorganize the state, to express not only their political interests as they related to the interests of the popular sectors, but also and more directly their own specific economic interests.

Populism and National Development

The development model in Brazil was different. Here the phase of outward expansion did not consolidate a hegemonic entrepreneurial sector that was strong and modern enough to neutralize the power of the traditional agricultural sectors, still less to unify the popular, rural, and urban sectors as a wage-earning mass. When substitutive industrialization began in the transition period, power was still in the hands of traditional oligarchy—a term used loosely to cover various segments of the exporting sector and of the non-exploiting latifundista groups. It was also shared with the middle groups with access to control of the state, the industrial bourgeoisie, and the urban merchants.

In Brazil, unlike in other countries that followed a liberal pattern of industrialization, the state emerged as an instrument not only to regulate the industrial system but also to directly participate in it through the creation of public enterprises, autarchic and state-controlled. In Brazil, unlike Argentina, a large sector of nonworker urban masses was added to the lesser weight of the worker sector. This difference became even more marked in the presence of a broad sector of rural masses living in a situation totally removed from that of the popular masses.

Populism appeared in Brazil as the link between the new scheme of power and the urban masses, who were either mobilized by industry or driven to the city by the decline of the agrarian sector. It was to change into a policy by which the masses participated politically in a relatively limited way, owing to their weak union structure. This policy affected neither the rural masses nor the whole of the urban popular sector.

Brazil lacked an agro-importing sector (that is, an economic sector limiting agro-export interests with trade import of industrial goods) that would have generated a significant subsidiary industrial economy. Substitutive industrialization was achieved, on the one hand, by direct state action and, on the other, by an industrial bourgeoisie largely unconnected with the agro-exporting sector. Not only did the state promote and even create the traditional branches of basic industry, it also participated in the initial development of industries of consumer durables such as automobiles, as well as industries of intermediate products such as cement or steel. These industrialization policies followed a line of "economic nationalism."[3] How could this type of orientation occur in a power situation where the basic political alliance embraced such diverse sectors—some of them very traditional—as landholding groups, urban popular sector, middle classes, and entrepreneurial groups of industry and commerce?

The answer is partly that the existing *private* groups capable of capitalizing industrial development were in a weaker economic position than in Argentina, for example, and were thus unable to impose a liberal industrialization policy. As industrialization gained momentum the agro-exporting groups lost control of the state apparatus to groups without common interests that could be satisfied through development of a liberal type.

The groups that reached power after 1930 were influenced more by political than by economic considerations in pursuing industrialization. Had they been influenced by economic considerations, they would have been concerned with forming a domestic market that would stimulate development and lead to self-sustained growth. But it was only at

3. See Carlos Lessa, "Dos experiencias de política económica: Brasil-Chile (una tentativa de confrontación)," *El Trimestre Económico*, 34, no. 135 (1967): 445–487.

a later date—when industrialization was well under way—
that they became interested in a policy of this kind.[4] So the
state's industrialization policy was not just thrust on it by the
force of economic circumstances—it was a political decision.

Government participation in the emergence of an industry can be explained politically by the existence of masses
that were mobilized without effective employment having
been created to absorb them. This caused a dangerous situation for those who held power. In an urbanizing country with
an agrarian economy in decline and a capitalist sector unable
to respond rapidly to massive employment requirements, it
was imperative that development be made a national undertaking—that is, one in the interest of all the people—and
that the state be charged with leading the nation to prosperity.

The alliance that was to carry out the new policy incorporated at the outset the most backward groups of landholders, the farmers who produced for the domestic market,
the urban middle class, the already existing industrial sectors,
and the urban mass. Not included were the agro-exporting
groups (coffee growers) that had controlled the system before
the 1930 revolution, or the rural masses. Although the former
were to join the "developmentalist alliance" later, the peasants were to be permanently excluded.

Domestic development in Brazil was supported politically by groups with conflicting interests. To create modern
economic sectors capable of employing the masses, it was
necessary to make a political alliance with the most backward
sectors of the Brazilian production structure, the non-export-
ing latifundistas. On the other hand, the viability of such a
policy of domestic development came to depend precisely on
a division between the urban mass that benefited from development and the rural mass that was marginal to it. The system of accumulation and economic expansion—given their

4. See F. H. Cardoso, *Empresário industrial e desenvolvimento
econômico no Brasil* (São Paulo: Difusão Europeia do Livro, 1964).

limited rate of growth—could not withstand the wage pressures that would result from incorporating broad rural sectors into the labor market. Moreover, the political strength of the landholding sectors depended on preventing the rural mass from receiving the benefits of economic, political, and social participation. Since the "developmentalist alliance" encompassed the hacendados, the alliance would be shattered by incorporating the peasants.

It was the excluded sectors that would pay the costs of industrialization. In the early stages, industrialization depended on the power of the state to tax the exporting sector and to exclude the rural and urban masses. Eventually, the export sector became diversified, and certain groups within it began to participate in development by reorienting their capital toward production for the domestic market. Nonetheless, because the rural mass continued to be isolated from the benefits of development, it constituted one of the structural limits to the political possibilities of development. Attempts to expand the "developmentalist alliance" with such groups were counterproductive, and populism could not be used as a base for legitimizing power.

The populism of Vargas was a rather vague movement of people's incorporation into the nation, but without entailing, as in the case of Perón, stronger trade unions and increased pressure for higher wages. It was less an economic definition of workers' rights, which would imply political participation, than a political movement in favor of the "humble." Since the emerging worker class was diluted in the urban mass, the need to accumulate capital did not seem to be much opposed to the pressures for redistribution during the phase of substitutive industrialization. Populist leadership could also be entrepreneurial; hence the state appeared not only as employer but also, from the viewpoint of the masses, even as a good employer. At the economic level, popular protest could be taken care of because it was relatively weak; at the political level, it coincided with the interests of groups that, having reached power without a solid economic base of their own, were in favor of development under state direction.

Even if this alliance favored nationalism and statism, it did not in any way exclude participation of the private sector, which—as the market was consolidated by the state—increasingly invested in the domestic economy. The private sector also needed the state as an instrument of bank-credit allocation and of income redistribution. But once the industrial sector was supported by a broader economic base and could get capital not only from the export sector but also from abroad, pressures rose against the inefficiency of the state as entrepreneur and against populism as a development policy. These pressures could be resisted by the urban middle classes, by the entrepreneurs who feared competition from efficient private monopolies, and by the private sectors organized around the state. But as soon as it became clear that intermediate and capital goods production and heavy industry would be controlled by either the state or big business (private monopolies), it was apparent that the populist scheme was too fragile to frustrate the hegemonic designs of the private groups. As the process of import substitution began to require better technology, higher accumulation, and more efficiency this became even clearer. Thus, populism and nationalism gave way to other social forces and to another political orientation of development.

It should be mentioned that the state was again briefly able to make populism its political line after the domestic market, now dominated by national and foreign private enterprise, had begun to be developed. The policy of the Goulart government was to try to broaden its base of support by organizing and incorporating peasant sectors as well as by expanding participation and economic benefits for the urban popular sector. Such an effort only demonstrated the impossibility of reconciling interests now clearly contradictory. Not only did it split off the apex of the nationalist-developmentalist alliance, the bourgeois and landholding sectors that were still committed to it, but it also jeopardized accumulation, mainly in the public sector: its social costs were high enough to put a drain on investment. Thus the limits of populism as a form of mobilization of the masses and as a development policy were reached.

The Developmentalist State

In an enclave economy, the domestic market expanded in the process of development. This transition required the state to allow broader political participation of the middle class and to enlist the support of the popular sectors for such a reorganization. In this sense, both the new industrial sectors and the popular sectors were either engaged in or associated with the state. The state promoted industrialization because the industrial sectors needed a mechanism of rapid capital accumulation, but it also did so because these industrial sectors represented an alliance between workers and middle groups, the middle groups being made up principally of the bureaucracy and the beginnings of the new bourgeoisie. This alliance could be maintained only by creating and expanding employment opportunities for the masses.

Such a situation occurred in Mexico and Chile. In Chile, for example, the urban economic sector that had formed in the previous phase continued to be important enough to try to control development or to use the favorable prospects for development for its own advantage. The popular sectors, because they were already established and organized, could try to impose their participation in development policies. In other words, the conflicts or alliances in the Chilean situation always involved class interests. There follows a discussion of how, in both Mexico and Chile, alliances and confrontations helped consolidate a policy of industrialization.

INDUSTRIALIZATION IN MEXICO

The new political power created by the Mexican Revolution (1910–1920) was seriously weakened by economic elements that the Revolution did not change. The basic sectors of the economy, transport,* mining, petroleum, and electric power, remained in the hands of foreign companies that were strong enough to restrain the Mexican government. Because of the destruction of the previous agrarian power structure, the peasants, although fervent defenders of the Revolution, were too dispersed to constitute a solid economic base for the revolutionary process. Nor could the workers, with their parallel and fragmented trade unions, bargain successfully with the foreign companies, much less contribute to government stability. The weakness of the system, then, was reflected in its lack of structure for political support from workers and peasants, and in the pressures put on it by an economy that was controlled from abroad.

The only way for the government to reinforce its position against the foreign companies was to organize and unite the worker-peasant movement. Having carried out this policy, Cárdenas (1934–1940) was able to challenge the foreign companies in the petroleum industry, which resulted in its nationalization.

The state, with popular support, began industrialization in Mexico. But its socialistic orientation alarmed not only foreign investors but also vast sectors of the national economy. Although everyone agreed on the need for industrialization, how and by whom was not clear. The relative national unity created by the revolutionary process was in jeopardy. A formula for industrial development was finally arrived at that welcomed foreign investment within limits set by the state. This policy was initiated by Avila Camacho and continued by Alemán. It was hoped that the economic development resulting from industrialization would make it possible to meet popular demands rapidly. Therefore, a large part of the industry established was subsidiary to the United States, which made investments in Mexico that benefited from the guarantees and facilities granted by the state itself. Foreign

*Although the Diaz government created a national administration for much of the Mexican railroad system, substantial parts remained under the control of foreign-owned companies.

investment flowed not only into industry but also into the financial and commercial sectors; the state saw to it that the new market was advantageous and, without intending to, helped create conditions for monopolistic operations.

The state continued to develop the basic structure and to ensure the best market conditions. It required only that industrial investors produce within the country. However, not only industrial activity but also agriculture began to attract foreign investment. The agrarian reform, and especially the ejidos, had provided the Revolution with political support. Now it became necessary also to integrate agriculture into an economic policy. The state carried out investments that improved agricultural productivity, but it began to favor the more capitalist sectors among the farmers, owing to the pressure it was under to create an agricultural base quickly. As had occurred in industry, foreign investment was encouraged in agriculture in order to accelerate development. The typical example was the cotton economy, where through market mechanisms the most developed groups began to dominate the noncapitalist producers.

A very close relationship was established between those who controlled the state politically and the new economic sectors. In this way, the fortune of the former came to depend on the growth capacity of the modern economic groups, both private and public. Nonetheless, it should be pointed out that urban popular sectors did not remain marginal. Perhaps the foregoing partly explains the continuance of a complex alliance among the most disparate social sectors.

THE CHILEAN CASE

After the 1929 crisis in nitrate, employment could only be maintained by state subsidies. With nitrate being replaced by chemical fertilizer on the world market, the foreign companies began to dismantle their plants. If balance was to be restored, a new economic structure had to be created to sustain it. During this period, the government took measures to expand or in some cases to create the industrial sector. The economic measures devised for this purpose were far from elaborate, but they had important effects. Perhaps the most far-reaching policy was that of exchange control, which forced the old importing sectors to invest their available capital in the national sphere, thereby creating industries that would replace former imports. Therefore, the state began to promote public works and other activities in order to generate employment; there could be no hope of resolving the existing unemployment by limited actions taken by the entrepreneurial sector. The creation of an import-substitution industry, and the direct intervention by the state to guide the economy, were two important consequences of the 1929 crisis.

Perhaps because of the weakness of the power structure, which only looked for new economic bases of support, politics appeared more often as a confrontation than as an alliance. The popular sectors were organized, had political representation, and were crucial elements for any new agreement. The middle sectors, especially those that in some way depended on the state, were also organized, and they aspired to an alliance that would permit them to share in power. The Popular Front (1937) sealed this possible alliance; to the middle and popular sectors were added some stronger economic and social groups that hoped to improve their position within the new order. With political power in its hands, the Popular Front began in 1939 a deliberate planning of the national economy through CORPO (Corporation to Promote Production), in which the state took an active part. One external factor, World War II, favored and to some degree even imposed the new policy by making it necessary to replace imports. Nevertheless, although the intention had been to plan the economy on a large scale, more work was done to create new activities, such as industrial development, electric power, and basic industries, than to modify existing activities.

In agriculture, a policy was proposed to diversify crops for export purposes, but this policy implied no change in the land tenure system and therefore none in the social order it supported. For industry the goal was to help form an industrial bourgeoisie through bank credits. Many industries, even those of foreign origin, could be installed and operated thanks to the facilities and guarantees furnished by the state. With renewed vigor, certain sectors of the existing bourgeoisie began to invest their capital in industry and to reinforce the commercial sector. The middle sectors, which largely managed the state apparatus, found in the revitalized bourgeoisie an ally that permitted them to resist popular and worker pressures. The development program promoted by this alliance was based on the willingness of the state to grant the new group bank credits and favorable conditions to operate in the market.

On the other hand, the external sector, now totally controlled by the United States, recovered. Copper replaced nitrate, and the state could count on revenue from this sector. Nevertheless, this recovery signified a slowdown in industrial development. The rate of growth in this sector declined, and in that sense there was stagnation.

Displacement of the popular sector as an ally produced serious political conflicts resulting in direct repression of the workers and especially the breakdown of their organized expression through the 1948 Ley de Defensa de la Democracia (Law of Democratic Defense). The middle sectors, by their turnabout, also left themselves in an extremely weak position with their recent allies. A new effort was made to reestablish their alliance with the popular sector, but in the absence of the political organizations that had formerly represented the various social sectors, the alliance as adopted took the form of a completely amorphous populism.

This populism—the first phase of the second government of Ibáñez—was of short duration, ending almost before the year was out. Its principal difficulty was to find a way to end Chile's runaway inflation. Orthodox measures to try to stabilize the situation were advised by the Klein-Sacks Mission and also were made a condition for external credit. With this policy the government lost its initial popular support.

The chaos of populism had an unexpected consequence in the restructuring of the political organizations representing the dissident factions. After the disappearance of populism, the new government thus clearly had a new socio-political character: the industrial, financial, and agrarian sectors bent their efforts to gain control of the domestic market. But they no longer did this through the state and even returned state economic activities to private capital. From a socio-political standpoint, the most notable feature of the regime of Jorge Alessandri (1958–1964) was the political polarization between the various social sectors.

CHAPTER SIX

The Internationalization of the Market

The New Nature of Dependence

In the formation of the domestic market, the impetus for industrialization was often maintained by a stable relationship between nationalism and populism. The diversification of the capitalist economy, however, was based on the creation of a capital-goods sector and a strengthening of the entrepreneurial groups; it was often accompanied by a crisis in populism and a political organization of dominant groups. This was also the period when efforts were first made to link the production sector oriented toward the domestic market to dominant external economies.

These efforts moved in two directions. On the one hand, they sought to transform the relation between the domestic economy and the hegemonic centers of the world market. The new factors influencing development, politics, and external dependence were not limited to the economic sphere, however; and it should not be concluded that once an advanced capitalist sector appeared in the dependent economies, economic determination of the political process permitted an immediate explanation of political life according to economic factors. Because dependence was still basic to the structure of the new development situation, politics continued to be the means by which economic determination was made possible. Because of the internal crisis the specifically political links in the relation between center and periphery were reinforced. The very structure of the production system, as well as the character of state and civil society, was reorganized to give way to a capitalist industrial system which could be developed both on the periphery of the world market and as an integral part of it.

The Structural Limits on the Process of National Industrialization

The preceding chapter described how a development alliance could try to broaden the base of the domestic economy, as occurred at different times in Argentina, Brazil, and Mexico. In these countries, power alliances were formed that smoothed the adjustment from old dominant situations to situations resulting from the emergence of the middle sectors, the industrial bourgeoisie and, to some extent, the urban masses. Although these alliances and combinations did not benefit their participants equally in every country, they did permit the accumulation that promoted domestic investment and expanded urban consumption. In these conditions, the state could channel the pressure of the popular classes and organized groups toward reaching an agreement favorable to development. The system could function only if export prices were maintained or even increased—as in the years during and immediately following World War II—so that broader urban industrial sectors of the economy could be financed without the profit level of the export sectors being lowered. The end of the export boom had different effects in each of the above countries, depending on the degree of progress in industrialization policies made possible by earlier political agreements.

In Argentina, where the agro-export sector continued to be economically important, industrialization, although accompanied by substantial redistribution, was not significant, especially in the basic industries.[1] The new situation of the world market presented the alternatives most dramatically: to hold down wages and public expenditures, at the expense of the worker-popular classes; or to reorganize and raise the productivity of the agro-export economy in order to use it to continue long-term financing of the modern industrial sector. After the fall of Perón in 1955, the anti-populist opposition chose the latter policy. Nevertheless, the export sector could not by itself impose this objective on the rest of the country, nor could it counteract the pressure of the masses through an alliance with the politically weak domestic industrial sectors, as was attempted by the Frondizi government (1958–1962). Military intervention became frequent both as a form of arbitration and as an open reaction against a return to populism. This course of economic development was vigorously blocked by broad sectors of wage earners. It could not be imposed as a policy that, if not legitimate, was at least efficient. Therefore, there was neither development nor political stability.

In Brazil, the Vargas scheme consisted in the installation of certain basic industries like steel, electric power, transport, and oil. This economic policy was continued during the Dutra

1. Altimir, Santamaría, and Sourrouille, "Los instrumentos de promoción industrial en la postguerra," *Desarrollo Económico* (Buenos Aires), vols. 21–25 (1966–1967).

government (1946–1950) although with another political base. During the second government of Vargas (1950–1954), the policy was more clearly directed toward a development stimulated by public investment in strategic sectors. This rapidly transformed the structure of urban production. Although the foreign exchange accumulated during the war years was not used altogether productively, Brazil's industrial plant was renewed, and heavy machinery continued to be imported against the prospect that the Korean crisis might lead to another world war. In this way a new boom was generated, and industrialization by domestic forces was accelerated.

Nevertheless, a political price had to be paid for this industrialization. The export sectors never ceased to protest state intervention in exchange control and multiple-exchange rates, which favored the domestic economy. Until 1953, the farmers could accept the policy of protection and rapid expansion of the domestic sector because their incomes were maintained by the export of coffee. When the price of coffee began to weaken on the world market in 1954, the Vargas alliance reached its limits. Part of the sector joined the urban middle class opposition, to which were added not only domestic but also international financial groups. A new fall in coffee prices was seized upon by the United States to bring pressure to bear on Vargas, whose nationalist policy had gone rather far.

After the suicide of Vargas, the populist developmentalist alliance was reestablished for a brief interim under Kubitschek. Kubitschek chose a course similar to the one Frondizi had tried to follow after years of stagnation in Argentina: capitalization with the aid of external resources. On a short-term basis, this policy reduced inflation and satisfied the wage demands of the modern urban groups; that is, it was an economic policy that was acceptable to the export sector and also strengthened the industrial sector, now associated with foreign capital. It could therefore promote development with political stability, in the short term.

In Mexico,[2] domestic production could be opened to foreign capital without provoking the kind of political-military crises that occurred in Brazil and Argentina. Not only had the state already defined its role as investor and regulator of the economy, thanks to which an urban financial-industrial bourgeoisie had been created, but the machinery for integration of trade unions had been modernized so that the worker-popular movement could participate in a society in which the state had legitimacy and a moderate policy of distribution.

In this way, the national bourgeoisie and the investor state did not come to a confrontation as they had in Brazil and Argentina, where the state had populist origins. The state itself did not turn radical; severe class conflicts did not arise; even the transition to a policy encouraging the participation of foreign capital did not meet with serious opposition. In these conditions, there could be development and stability.[3]

Nevertheless, the price of this development was the gradual building up of a new kind of oligarchy, which manipulated the state for its own benefit and to advance its scheme of development in association with foreign capital. Thus what could have been a modernized social and political development came to the dead end of the present state of capitalist development in Latin America: modernization at the cost of growing authoritarianism and continuing poverty typical of "development with marginal population."[4]

The foregoing observations do not attach any inevitability to capitalist development through external control or participation; nor do they imply the opposite belief that would

2. See Pablo González Casanova, *La democracia en México* (Mexico: Ediciones Era, 1965).
3. See ECLA, *Estudio Económico,* 1966.
4. "Marginal population" in the Latin American context means people without stable occupation. Behind this notion lies the

make historical chance the only explanation. On the contrary, this interpretation proposes that there are necessary structural limitations on a nationally controlled industrial development within which the various social forces operate.

The conflicts or agreements among these different forces are not subject to determinism. In specific situations, their interactions may result in historical events that are absolutely different from the ones analyzed here, as in the case of Cuba. But to the extent that the system of social relations is expressed through a system of power, a combination of structural possibilities is established historically. Within the framework of the structural possibilities engendered by earlier social practices, certain courses are indicated and other alternatives are excluded.

Structurally, industrialization in Latin America requires vast accumulation and, in turn, produces marked social differentiation. The nature of investment for this type of development is in conflict with the pressures of the various sectors to gain participation.

Inward development in Latin America depended on an improvement in the terms of trade and on some participation by the population in the benefits of development. Momentarily favorable circumstances made it possible to incorporate the masses without excluding the dominant sectors and strata of the period of outward expansion. This incorporation took place through the national populist version of the "developmentalist alliance" in Brazil under Vargas, and in Argentina under Perón, and through the "developmentalist state" in Mexico. When an attempt was made to satisfy the pressures

---

assumption that capitalistic growth, even when implying industrialization, cannot meet the demands of the masses for jobs and well-being. We know that sustained periods of growth do expand labor markets. But taking into account economic cycles and structural heterogeneity in Latin American societies, it is worthwhile to stress that poverty problems are not being solved through capitalistic industrialization.

from the peasant and urban popular sectors for greater incorporation, the capacity of accumulation was lowered. This broke an important link in the alliance of political hegemony: the agrarian sectors, especially the latifundista, turned against those urban industrial sectors that might support the demands of the masses; at the same time, the agrarian groups found allies in the industrial and financial groups that could not meet the pressures of the urban popular sectors for higher wages. Moreover, if world conditions were unfavorable, the farmers opposed any attempt by the state or the urban industrial society to transfer income from the agrarian to the urban sector.

Exports continue to be vital to development because they make possible accumulation and industrial financing, but their prospects on the world market are beyond national control. Hence the downward trend in the terms of trade is an additional limitation on the structural possibility of development.

The political dynamic of nationalist populism or of the "developmentalist state" as a power base requires state intervention to maintain wage levels and even to raise them —for example, when mass support or broader consumption is called for. Urban industrial growth also requires, at least in the phase of import substitution, greater incorporation of the masses, if not in relative terms, certainly in absolute numbers. All this intensifies popular pressures, which become dangerous to the system when they coincide with a fall in export prices or with a spurt of inflation that accelerates a transfer of income away from the rich.

When a political crisis in the system prevents an economic policy of public and private investment for development, the only alternatives are opening the market to foreign capital or making a radical political move toward socialism. This is shown by an examination of the prevailing political structure.

Suppose that the national industrial sector controls the state. Industrialization might conceivably be carried out in this situation through the following policies:

1. By keeping up export prices in order to continue the transfer of income to other sectors. But this would be manifestly impossible as a policy, because prices are determined outside the sphere of the national economy; its very impossibility is one of the limits of the development model.

2. By a confrontation with the agro-export sector in order to continue the transfer of income from it to other sectors. This not only would involve a profound change in the scheme of agreements, but also would affect the main source of its financing, which would tend to diminish.

3. By holding down wages and stepping up capital investments, this could, in addition to disrupting the system of political agreements, lead to a confrontation with organized labor and also reduce domestic consumption.

4. By lessening urban popular participation. This could build up popular pressures and create a political crisis within the scheme of power support.

5. By closing the domestic market to foreign capital and imports. This would signify a kind of declaration of moratorium on the foreign debt and, consequently, a confrontation with the external factors of dominance.

6. By excluding the agrarian sector and intensifying regional disparities. Although this might cause conflict, it would not necessarily cause a profound crisis in the political system.

Suppose, on the other hand, that the crisis will be faced by the populist state itself. Suppose, that is, that popular leaders as well as the urban industrial bourgeoisie are present in the power structure, and that the masses are prepared to defend the state. Even here, development still would not be possible without radical political changes or the acceptance of foreign penetration into the domestic market. In addition to the confrontations listed under the first hypothesis, the opposition aroused by a wage control and diminished popular participation would be replaced by new confrontations inside the populist state itself. The popular sectors would not remain in the alliance without exerting further pressure for income redistribution; and the entrepreneurial sectors, both public and private, could not accede to such pressure and still continue to capitalize and invest.

Most radically opposed to populism would be a scheme based on an alliance between the industrial bourgeoisie and the agro-exporting bourgeoisie. There are possibilities of conflict here as well. The agro-export sector would not be a good ally to resist pressure in favor of opening the investment market, since foreign investment generates an industrialization that does not depend chiefly on taxes from the national export sector as a source of capital formation. Furthermore, urban worker opposition would disrupt the scheme or carry it to a political dead end, since otherwise workers would have to bear the cost of accumulation.

So the possibilities just explored have been actively tried out, although not in pure form.

The Opening of Domestic Markets to External Control

The foregoing explains why attempts to maintain the rate of industrialization cannot succeed without profound political-structural changes. What has not been made clear is that foreign industrial capital was searching for new markets. This search became connected with internal interests in a way that was acceptable at least to those in power.

In the 1950s, international capital movements were characterized by brief periods of capital flow from center to periphery. Unlike the previous scheme of investment by banks, industrial corporations became investors, and there was demand for new investments.

The early phase of substitutive industrialization and consolidation of the domestic market had been one of public and private internal accumulation, which was encouraged by protectionist policies.[5] These policies were precisely what led

5. Santiago Macario, *Proteccionismo e industrialización en América Latina* (mimeographed document presented to the Second Regional Course in Trade Policy, Santiago, 1967).

the foreign supplier of manufactured products to invest in the peripheral economies so as to get around the tariff wall. His investments were of two kinds. The first were those which took advantage of an already existing market and in that sense competed with the internal industrial sectors, often subordinating them to his interests. This can be seen in the relation between the automobile industry and the national industries manufacturing replacement parts. The second were those which assured him virtual control of an expanding market.

While import substitution was growing, the penetration of foreign capital was not regarded as a development problem even though it marginalized certain domestically owned industries. In fact, internal industrial sectors had new fields for investment:[6] each manufactured product stimulated the progressive replacement of its parts and components, until the point was reached where the only products that had to be imported were those that required a very advanced technology or primary materials that did not exist in the country.[7] Furthermore, through this process certain worker sectors and other technical-professionals were incorporated into the industrial economy, which helped maintain the "developmentalist alliance," in this case excluding the populist forms. This temporary coincidence of political and economic interests made it possible to reconcile protectionist policies, part of the popular pressure, and foreign investment. Thus foreign investment was a basic condition for development.

Industrialization was based on an urban market. While it intensified the exclusive social system characteristic of capitalism in peripheral communities, it nonetheless promoted

6. This explains the internal mobility of the entrepreneurial sectors; in this connection, see Luciano Martins, "Formação do empresariado no Brasil," *Revista do Instituto de Ciencias Sociais,* vol. 3, no. 2.

7. Maria da Concieção Tavares, "Substitucao de importacoes e desenvolvimento na America Latina," *Dados* (Rio de Janeiro), vol. 1, no. 1, pp. 115–140.

capital accumulation and increasing complexity in the production structure.[8]

This process was compatible with the power relations among the competing social classes—until easy import substitution ceased. From this moment, when the substitution process slowed down, it became apparent that the technologically and economically more significant manufactures of intermediate and capital goods had created complex problems that had been postponed by the euphoria of development. Not only did the organizations of productions need to regroup internally and strengthen the ties between national enterprises and foreign monopolistic groups, but the growing pressures of the social sectors that had not been included in this scheme needed to be taken into account. Industrial sectors that had emerged in the early stages of substitution now became marginal; there were protests from these. Urban popular sectors tried to revive a state development policy as a defense against the large private production units oriented toward more productivity and less use of labor. This was the breakdown of the old "developmentalist alliance."

Divisions now began to appear in the structure of social classes: a more modern versus a more traditional proletariat; an entrepreneurial sector that controlled high-productivity industry using advanced technology versus a traditional sector that had been established during the stage of easy import substitution.

Dependence and Development

The integration into the world market of the industrial-peripheral economies was different from that of the agro-export economies. The same was true of the political expression of this integration.

---

8. For a description of the effects of this type of industrialization on the structure of employment, see Cardoso and Reyna, *Industrialización, estructura ocupacional y estratificación social en América Latina* (Santiago: ILPES, 1966).

The peripheral economies were linked to the international market at the time when the center of capitalism no longer acted solely through control of the import-export system, but acted also through direct industrial investment in the new national markets. Studies on external financing in Latin America made it clear that foreign investment was increasingly directed to the manufacturing sector through private investment—with direct investment predominating over portfolio investment—and that it operated through a very small number of firms.[9]

Latin American industrialization was launched during the Great Depression and was promoted by internal social forces, so it could not have been the result of the industrial expansion of the center. But there is no doubt that the direct participation of foreign enterprise gave a special cast to the development of industries in the Latin American periphery. During the nationalist-populist period, both national producing groups and the state consolidated centers of production. However, a development pattern was chosen that depended on increasing amounts of foreign investment in the industrial sector.

This kind of development situation engenders specific relations between internal growth and external ties. Although dependence imposed by external financing is characterized by an expanding, mainly short-term debt, dependence under monopolistic industrial capitalism acquires features that distinguish it from previous basic situations of underdevelopment.

In terms of diversification of production, levels of development may seem very high. But both capital flow and economic decisions are controlled from abroad. Even when production and marketing are carried out within the dependent economy, earnings go to swell capital funds available

9. Cf. ECLA, *El financiamiento externo de América Latina* (New York: United Nations, 1964), especially pp. 225–238. It should be mentioned that in 1950 slightly more than 300 enterprises owned 91 percent of all direct investment by the United States in Latin America (p. 238).

to the central economies. Investment decisions also depend in part on external considerations and pressures. Decisions taken by the parent companies, which only partly reflect the domestic market situation, significantly influence the reinvestment of profits generated in the national system. In certain circumstances, firms can opt to transform their profits into capital for investment in the central economies or in other dependent economies.

Most similarities between the dependence situation of the industrialized peripheral economies and that of the enclave economies are superficial. The industrialized economy requires a highly diversified output; a relatively low outflow of profits in order to safeguard reinvestment, especially in the capital goods sector; use of skilled labor and growth of a tertiary sector; a more balanced income distribution in the urban industrial sector; and as a consequence, a domestic market capable of absorbing output.

It might be said that what occurs here is the opposite of what happens in an enclave economy; for while investment decisions depend, if only partly, on the domestic market, consumption is domestic. In the most typical cases, there is a strong trend to local reinvestment, which means that in a certain sense foreign industrial investments and the domestic market are unified by an administrative, technological, and financial reorganization that in turn brings about a reordering of the forms of social and political control.

Even in this case it is not the advanced technology itself or the flow of new external capital into the economy that encourages or guides the course of development. Political arrangements are required for the economic evolution and the overall dynamic of societies. A modern process of industrialization in the peripheral nations requires vast capital input, a large store of technological knowledge, and a highly skilled managerial organization. These in turn require scientific development, a complex and differentiated social structure, and previous accumulation and investment. The fact that the central nations have these available tightens the bonds of dependence.

There are examples of underdeveloped nations that have tried, sometimes successfully, to reorient the production system while preserving a reasonable degree of autonomy. When development and autonomy are achieved simultaneously, resources and economic and organizational creativity located within the nation have been mobilized. Political conditions have made this possible. In the cases of the Soviet Union and China, there was a period of relative economic isolation through a partial closing of the market, which blocked pressures to expand consumption of the goods and services typical of mass industrial societies. In general, there was a broadening of state control over the production system as well as a channeling of new investment toward sectors considered strategic to national development. Such sectors were those of infrastructure or advanced technology, or even those connected with national defense. All this required a corresponding reorganization of the social system, a relatively authoritarian discipline (even in cases like Japan where a capitalist regime was maintained), and a revolution in national goals, including the priorities of education.

This was not the course followed by Latin America as it attempted to enter the era of modern industrial production. Some countries of the region have managed to accelerate industrialization through the transfer of foreign capital together with advanced technology and organization for production. But they have done this at the expense of the autonomy of the national economic system and of policy decisions for development.

Competition in the open market, standards of industrial quality and productivity, size of investment (for example, to install the petro-chemical industry), patterns of consumption —all these impose certain forms of organization that affect the overall economy. In this sense, the capital, technology, and organization transferred from the external sector create a reordered economy.

When not directed by the national society, this transformation entails another, more complex dependence. The state can react to the pressures of the external market by using political instruments such as monetary and employment policies and in this way safeguard part of national autonomy in investment and consumption decisions. But in this new type of development, some of the mechanisms controlling the national economy are beyond the control of the country concerned; the international market sets certain universal standards for the modern production system that allow no alternatives. Unification of production systems under the control of multinational corporations leads to market regulation and supranational organization.

The new situation is more involved than in previous cases. Domestic capital formation goes through a cycle: output, marketing, consumption, financing, business savings, reinvestment; insofar as this cycle is completed in terms of large production units, the economic system tends to impose its norms on the society, thereby limiting the effectiveness of the autonomous counterweight of the local groups.

Of course, in the industrialized countries of Latin America like Mexico and Brazil, where the public sector participates in economic regulation and formation of new capital, a greater measure of autonomy of internal decisions can be attained. The earlier forms of organization and control of production, even as regards dependence, do disappear from the scene. All this leads to an increasingly complex political life.

In this new form of development, the public sector, the multinational corporation, and the modern capitalist sector of the national economy are joined. This union requires an adequate system of relations among the groups controlling the different economic sectors, and it requires the economic action of these various groups to be possible politically. In this form of development, it is assumed that market growth is based on closer relations among producers, who become the most important "consumers" in the economic expansion: each enterprise sells machines and final goods to the other. To raise the accumulation or savings capacity of these "producer-consumers," the demands of the masses must be contained, and as a consequence, a policy of redistribution to broaden consumption becomes ineffective and even contrary to this type of development based on the dynamism of big enterprises.

In these conditions, political instability increases to the extent that consolidation of the state depends on the electoral game. This game becomes more difficult to play as the flow of foreign investments declines and the terms of trade deteriorate.

The dynamism of the modern sector is based on almost automatic mechanisms. Local industries become dependent on foreign technology and require a continuous expansion. These conditions make it hard for the government to support some of the older national industries that emerged during the import-substitution period or to choose labor-intensive policies for development.

Thus, development accentuates the social exclusion not only of the masses but also of the social strata that were economically important in the earlier stage and that are now obliged to try to find a subordinate place in the modern monopolistic sector and in the system of political domination. Although there is the possibility of modernizing the industrial sector and of diversifying it through the international monopolistic production unit, these "islands of modern industry" are inserted into a context in which the old agro-exporting society with its two subgroups (agro-commercial and latifundista), the industrial groups formed before the monopolistic predominancy, the middle groups, and the populace with its subdivisions (rural and urban masses and the working class) are always present and trying to define their solidarity with the proposed socio-economic order in a way that will assure them some share in development. Because the rest of the economy is underdeveloped, the modern industrial and the industrialized agrarian sectors can barely hold their ground or can expand only slowly. They lack the dynamism needed to "modernize" society as a whole. Their capacity to incorporate is restricted by their technological base; and their market problem is taken care of by a narrow system of trade between producers and buyers in which the state continues to be the principal buyer and retains an important role as producer.

Participation of the masses, especially in the economy, depends on how much the public sector of the economy developed in the earlier phase and, above all, on how much control the state exercised over the modern monopolistic sectors. Even in this case, those who control the state sector of the economy come to act more as public entrepreneurs than as implementers of a populist policy to promote income redistribution through steady wage increases. In this aspect, the state ceases to be a populist state and is transformed into an entrepreneurial state.

In a country like Mexico, where the popular sector as well as the entrepreneurial sector are already within the state apparatus and closely related to the system of political decisions, there is not only a gradual reorganization in keeping with the new development situation, but also an almost formal definition of the sphere of influence of these sectors and that of the sector linked to foreign forms. On the other hand, in countries like Argentina and Brazil, the transition is complicated because the state has liberal roots which make difficult the corporate control of economic decisions. A reorganization of the state's functions is required to give it increasing authority to regulate the economy. Furthermore, the dominant groups try to make the regime itself more authoritarian and centralized. This helps consolidate their domination as well as establish the capitalist mode of production in the dependent economies.

Opposition to this reorganization might find support in the social classes most directly affected by the exploitation: the marginal masses and the workers whose living standards suffer under the new stage of capitalist accumulation, the leftist parties, the liberal intellectuals, and the nationalist sectors. The opposition would also be based on private groups not involved with the foreign monopolistic sector, who ideally would try to remake the "downward" alliance in order to improve their position for political negotiation with the new dominant group.

Theoretically, in countries where the modern production sector was established under the aegis of the new conditions of development and dependence, it should have been possible to reorganize the system of political decisions and to reorient the economy in a way consistent with the interest of big corporations as exemplified by the Castelo Branco–Roberto Campos program in Brazil. Serving as background for the economic and political changes were the dynamic of international relations and especially the ideology of national security founded on belief in the imminence of a third world war, as well as on the preponderant role of the Western alliance and the consequent subordination of national interests to the bloc headed by the United States, and on the form adopted by the conflict between East and West in which the "external enemy" coexisted with the "internal enemy": guerrillas are conceived as the invisible hand of the Soviets.

There is no doubt that the new type of development requires renovation of the socio-political system. It requires a structure of domination that is not, or is only partly, based on the landholding and exporting sectors or on those sectors linked to industries of nondurable consumer goods. The new economic sector, controlled by the multinational corporations and the recently emerged financial sector linked to the domestic market, tries to influence national decisions. This goal is reached with difficulty, with factional disputes within the sector, and with opposition from other classes in the power game. Furthermore, insofar as the public sector has acquired importance in the economy, the state has room to manipulate the formation of new power alliances.

This last point is crucial. The democratic-representative regime, which in one form or another survived under the developmentalist state and under the populist policy of the initial phase of industrial expansion, is converted into the authoritarian-corporative regime through rebellions in which large national organizations like the army and the public bureaucracy (rather than the national or internationalized bourgeoisie) take action and reorganize. Of course, because the structural system that limits the possible action of these groups has not changed, the internationalized bourgeoisie continues to be the basis of the system of domination. Nevertheless, in Latin America from the transition period on, the political expression of the urban industrial bourgeoisie—unlike that of the earlier agro-exporting bourgeoisie—has been more directly linked to the state, through pressure groups and posts within the state apparatus, than to parties of class interests. In the same way, wage earners have been organized more as union members, under state tutelage, than as militant party members. The exception to the rule is Mexico; and even in this case, the party has been the political expression of the state itself, within which the classes occupy positions that are defined almost corporatively.

The crisis of developmentalist populism in Argentina as in Brazil led to the mobilization of the bourgeoisie and of the intermediate strata against the "Communist peril," against internal subversion, and against popular pressures on the state (actual, in the case of Goulart; potential, in the case of Perón's possible return to the government). The form adopted to repel democratic power was the military coup. However, the significance of these military takeovers, and of their factional countercoups, was different from what had occurred in the past with the military caudillos. At present, the armed forces occupy the state as a technobureaucratic corporation to serve what they believe to be the best interest of the nation. The traditional political sectors, which within the state expressed class domination in the developmentalist-populist period, have been eliminated; military influence is advanced as a necessary condition for development and national security; and military interference in economic, political, and social life is dressed up to appear as a kind of technocratic arbitration. In this way, there has come about a partial fusion of the two large organizations that effectively and permanently control the whole country: the armed forces and the state bureaucracy.

Organized groups are important in relatively unstructured underdeveloped societies; so the military and state bureaucracies have inevitable political advantages in the Latin American situation. It is nevertheless difficult for the civil society to accept the authoritarian-corporative regime.

The technobureaucracy of dependent countries is based on the decision-making and organizational potential of the modern sectors and the military and civil bureaucracy. In the process of its formation, it is subjected to two types of pressure: one, from big business, advocating rational modern development promoted by the large, generally internationalized financial-industrial corporations; the other, calling attention to the increasingly exclusive character of capitalist development in dependent countries and to the national character of the tasks to be accomplished and the problems to be solved in the course of development. This second point of view finds support even in sections of the armed forces and state technocracy. Consequently, segments of the military-bureaucratic axis often consider topics, such as agrarian reform, income redistribution, and balanced regional development, that disregard the preponderance of the capitalist-dependent structure of the local economy and appear to belong more properly to the earlier period of development. Within the civil and military bureaucracies, there are also supporters, often powerful, for the middle-class ideologies that believe economic policy should favor an equitable growth of the economy and of income and that the state should be a forum for mediation of class and group interests.

So the struggle among classes and groups does not end even within the dominant bureaucracies. It is unlikely, of course, that the nationalist-reformist policies can have more than momentary success. But the bourgeoisie do not have specifically political organizations, and their control of the state is at present almost purely structural. It is only when the policies of the militarized technobureaucracy clash with the mechanisms of capitalist accumulation and expansion that the entrepreneurial groups seek to correct nationalist deviations. Meanwhile, the sectors that carry out the reforms in the name of the nation, above class interests, have some justification for believing that they can transform their ideology into universal truth.

In the face of these unresolved conflicts, the economic transformations in the new scheme of power continue to be developmentalist, without necessarily excluding control of the economy by foreign monopolies.

The other extreme of reaction to the system of power is based on the opposition of the wage-earning classes and the "marginal groups" that are growing in number because of the form assumed by capitalist development in the periphery. Actually, the modern industrial system increases marginalization. This makes it more difficult to channel popular pressures through existing organized structures like trade unions, political parties, and the state. How these new popular masses are to be mobilized remains unknown. They present a broad range of alternatives of political action—from the creation of centers of insurrection to the reconstitution of the mass popular movement.

The weakness of the attempts to transform the status quo through mobilization of the unincorporated masses is due in part to the lack of structure of these masses and to their poverty and low level of expectations. In part it is also due to the divisions among the wage-earning sectors created by the new bases of development and dependence. The wage-earning groups linked to the advanced capitalist sector benefit from development and to some extent cushion the pressure from below; their demands become dissociated from the mass popular pressures.

In the context of the authoritarian-corporative domination the accomplishments of the political pressures of the wage earner are modest, even those of wage earners belonging to the advanced capitalist sector. Their gains will depend on improvement in union organization and on differentiation of the middle classes into sectors more directly linked to the capitalist-industrial mode of production. This last change includes modernizing the organization that is usually the spearhead of the middle class in the political game: the university with its technical institutes, which offers the specialized knowledge that will give prestige to professionals and technicians in the new society. Such changes may help the middle class to recover their influence on political and economic decisions.

It would be risky to argue that this change in the political participation of some sectors of wage earners and the middle class into greater integration into the new system of domination is a definite trend. The Latin American political experience indicates, rather, that in times of political protest, classes demonstrate "horizontal" solidarity, as exemplified by the copper and tin miners, as well as by the workers in state enterprises, who are usually better paid and also more politicized.

Behind the political struggles set in motion by conditions of confrontation between classes there are contradictions. There are general contradictions engendered by a production system based on large monopolistic units, and specific contradictions engendered by a capitalist development originating in the dominant centers of international capitalism. Consequently, at this moment in history, the central themes of development are the formation of a supranational market in which an economy of scale can function, and of a domestic market in which the possibilities of mass consumption are restricted; authoritarian-corporative reorganization of the political regime in an attempt to maintain stability in a mass society, but without including popular participation; and accumulation and higher concentration of capital in a structure of concentrated incomes.

Working against time, the new system of power tries to consolidate itself against the inroads of the opposition. The transition to a capitalist-industrial mode of production in dependent countries is managed by authoritarian political regimes (military or civilian), whose survival will depend not only on their achievements in economic development and social reconstruction but also on the type of action and the strength of the opposition.

Conclusions

From a methodological standpoint, we attempt to reconsider the problems of economic development through an interpretation emphasizing the political character of the processes of economic transformation. At the same time, we try to demonstrate that the historical situation in which the economic transformations occur must be taken into account if these changes as well as their structural limitations are to be understood.

This formulation of the relation between economic process, structural conditions, and historical situations makes clear that theoretical schemes concerning the formation of capitalist society in present-day *developed* countries are of little use in understanding the situation in Latin American countries. Not only the historical moment but also the structural conditions of development and society are different.

Recognizing these differences, we go on to criticize the concepts of underdevelopment and economic periphery and to stress both the economic aspects of underdevelopment and the political process by which some countries dominate others. We stress the specificity of installations of capitalist production in dependent societies.

We return to the tradition of political thought that there is no metaphysical relation of dependence between one nation and another, between one state and another. These relations are made possible through a network of interests and coercions that bind some social groups to others, some classes to others. This being the case, it is necessary to determine the way in which state, class, and production are related in each basic situation of dependence.

To characterize these relations, we show that Latin American class relations can be defined both in terms of the relationship between the production system and the international market and in terms of the form of control of production. Defining class relations in these ways reveals two basic historical situations. In one case, we point to the specificity of the enclave economies; in the other, to national control of the export system.

We go on to indicate how these historical transformations occur in particular social formations, and we avoid the two fallacies frequently found in similar interpretations: a belief that the internal or national socio-political situation is mechanically conditioned by external dominance; and the opposite idea that all is due to historical contingency. In fact, even the relation of dependence does not mean that national history in dependent nations will simply reflect changes in the external hegemonic center, although these changes are relevant to the possible autonomy of national history. There are structural limits to possible action, beginning with the available material base of production and the degree of development of the forces of production, and including the way in which these are combined with political and juridical relations within the country and its link with the hegemonic countries. Through the actions of groups, classes, organizations, and social movements in the dependent countries, these links are perpetuated, modified, or broken. Therefore, there is an internal dynamic that explains the course of events and thereby makes possible a political analysis.

We show how the different structural possibilities of an enclave situation and of a situation in which the export system is nationally controlled affect the social, political, and economic changes that take place in the countries under consideration.

In the final chapters we return to the general topic of the structural conditions of capitalist development in dependent countries. We characterize the contradictions between the pattern of dependent industrialization and the interests of the nation, as well as the conflicts in the relations among classes and social groups and between the latter and the state.

We also try to show the relative autonomy, the conflict, and the possibilities of convergence between the economic system and the political process. We point out that for an understanding of the present situation of the industrialized and dependent countries of Latin America, an analysis is required of the increasing control over the economic system of nations by large multinational corporations.

The originality of the hypothesis is not in its recognition of the existence of external domination—an obvious process. It is in its description of the form and the effects of this type of dependence on classes and state with reference to past situations. The present situation of dependent development goes beyond the traditional dichotomy between the terms "development" and "dependence," because it permits an increase in development while maintaining and redefining the links of dependency. The present situation is supported politically by a system of alliances that are different from those that previously assured external hegemony. It is no longer the exporting interests that subordinate the interests associated with the domestic market, nor rural interests that oppose urban ones as an expression of economic domination. The specificity of the present situation of dependence is in part that internal interests are rooted more and more in the sector producing for the domestic market and thus that they are united in political alliances that are supported by urban populations. The formation of an industrial economy in the periphery of the capitalist system minimizes the effects of the typically colonial exploitation; this economy incorporates not only the dominant classes but also social groups tied to modern capitalist production, such as wage earners, technicians, entrepreneurs, and bureaucrats.

The great political movements that try to form and strengthen the domestic market and the national economy—populism and nationalism—lose meaning in the new situation of dependence.

We speculate how far dependence can be maintained within the transformation described, or whether it will have to be replaced by interdependence. In this connection, we analyze the specificity of the structural situation together with the political situation. It is shown that the power interests and the alliances to guarantee the hegemony of internal and external groups and class factions have to be considered if the situation of diversification of the economic system is to be explained.

The basic economic conditions of development are an open market, the exclusion of the dependent economies from the markets of the most developed countries, and the continuous transfer of new units of external capital in the form of advanced technology, which are more appropriate to the intrinsic needs of the mature economies than to those of the relatively backward economies. The combination of these conditions with the ideologies and legal relations among social groups makes possible "industrial economies in dependent societies." Whether the structural barriers to development remain or are overcome will be determined by how these economic conditions are used in the power game rather than by the particular economic conditions themselves. In this sense, we suggest that present or potential opposition may vitalize the industrialized and dependent countries of Latin America. There are structural possibilities for various types of social and political movements.

The course of history depends largely on the daring of those who propose to act in terms of historically viable goals. We do not try to place theoretical limits on the probable course of future events. These will depend, not on academic predictions, but on collective action guided by political wills that make work what is structurally barely possible.

Post Scriptum

Although ten years have elapsed since this book was written, we have maintained its original structure and interpretations, for any attempt to bring it up to date would be futile. We have not dealt with all the historically significant situations that occurred in Latin America, nor have we emphasized the description of specific events or circumstances. Rather, we only wished to delineate the main tendencies of the historical-structural development. Moreover, the last ten years have been too rich in significant events for us to have the illusion that we could summarize them in a few additional pages.

The main theme of our essay is the relationship that exists between political struggles of groups and classes, on

This chapter was written for the English edition of the book *Dependencia y Desarollo en América Latina (Dependency and Development in Latin America)*; it was translated by Victoria Garcia.

the one hand, and the history of economic-political structures of domination, both internal and external, on the other.
Thus, it is of less interest to us to catalogue events than to
seek in them the meaning of basic structural relationships
and the stages of their development in their double determination: on the level of local systems of domination and
on the level of their relationship with the international order.
Political and economic processes appear in the latter as if they
were the expression of a struggle between nation-states, but
they also involve conflicts between social groups and classes.

In order to explain the historical process from the theoretical perspective of dependence, we must make explicit how
international conflicts between states are linked with internal
political struggles as well as with the basic ways whereby,
both domestically and internationally, the social organization
of economic production takes place.

It should be enough to mention some of the important
events in Latin American history to suggest that certain fundamental transformations took place in the world during the
last ten years, and that those changes were not merely epi-
sodic but rather reflect a change in the structural relationships
between the two great contemporary socio-economic systems,
capitalism and socialism, as well as within each of them:

—the stabilization and progress of the Cuban socialist
regime;

—the "capitalist road" of development, such as mani-
fested itself in the Brazilian "economic miracle," accompanied by a military regime;

—the experiment of the "electoral road" to socialism in
Chile and the "destabilization" practices initiated by the
capitalist order to destroy it;

—Peruvian military reformism and the attempts at
autonomy, under military regimes, in Panama (and, more
episodically, in Bolivia under Torres and in Ecuador between
1972 and 1975);

—the arduous road of guerrilla efforts which, although
begun before the last ten years, were militarily and politically

defeated only recently in Peru, Venezuela, Guatemala, Bolivia, Santo Domingo, Brazil, and Uruguay;

—the persistence of an embryonic state of popular-guerrilla insurrections in Argentina before and after the second Peronist government, and of guerrilla nuclei of lesser importance in Colombia and Nicaragua, as well as the emergence of unexpected forms of protest against the dominant order in Mexico since the student movement that led to the tragic episode of Tlalteloco;

—the emergence of Caribbean countries in the Latin American political scene, with Guyana's popular-autonomist strategies, the repressive-enlightened traditionalism of Trinidad-Tobago, and the attempts at articulation between these countries and Jamaica;

—Honduras's populist militarism, its war with El Salvador, and the "stability" of the rest of the area, including Guatemala and Nicaragua;

—the same "stabilization" in the Caribbean, both in the Dominican Republic and in Haiti, after the family succession;

—the persistence of caudillo-style militarism in Paraguay, reinforced by alliances with Brazil (a process anticipating the direction Bolivia would take after General Banzer's coup);

—finally, almost like an archeological find, the survival of traditional bipartisan elitist democracy in Colombia, and the shakier experimentation with partisan and democratic practices in Venezuela, which, because of oil, has presented the most spectacular rate of economic growth in the area;

—and one might mention the political movements in colonial areas such as Puerto Rico, the Guianas, and several islands and enclaves in the Caribbean, including the Panama Canal Zone.

This bird's-eye view of recent history should suffice to indicate that one or even several new books would be necessary to replace the facile adjectives used above with an analysis of the historical processes involved.

Even so it seems necessary to refer in this *post scriptum* to the basic tendencies underlying those processes. We shall limit ourselves to a discussion of three general topics: the great changes in the capitalist system and in the international order; the implications for international politics of Latin American participation in world affairs; and the reorganization of the internal political order, especially of the state, in Latin America, together with the reaction of popular movements.

The Reorganization of World Economic Order and Multinational Corporations

In chapter six we considered the effects of the penetration of multinational corporations into Latin American countries. What was but a trend ten years ago is today a marked fact, not only in Latin America but also throughout the fringes of the capitalist world. However, we believe that this phenomenon—the preeminence of multinational corporations—should be analyzed in a global perspective that gives due value to the role of politics in the reorganization of the international economic order. It would be an error, according to the approach proposed in this book, to analyze those political transformations independently from the dynamics of the capitalist system as a whole. The system, in turn, evolves on an international level, and thus it is continuously faced with the presence and the challenge created by the existence of socialist economies and countries. It is therefore necessary to make an effort to understand the predominance and the limitations of international corporations within this wider context.

We shall attempt to clarify only three points in this topic: the significance of the reorganization of world capitalism for central economies; the effects of this process on peripheral economies; and finally the relationships between this process and the national state.

The first question is essential to an understanding of some of the difficulties in the contemporary international

economy. After World War II this economy expanded under
the uncontested hegemony of the American economy. This
process of expansion was rooted in the impact of the American military victory, in the instability of the national states
in postwar Europe, as well as in the drain caused by the war
effort on the Soviet economy. It was also based on the intrinsic dynamism typical of an oligopolistic economy of large
enterprises, and was supported by important technological
achievements that were accelerated by the war. The relative
advantages of the American economy were undeniable: the
political and military predominance of the United States was
made manifest by atomic supremacy; technological capacity
and the increased introduction on the market of new products that could hardly be rivaled reinforced the initial advantage and assured the United States umistakable leadership
in the capitalist world. The value of the dollar and its adoption as reserve currency reflected that reality. Control of international economy by the United States was insured by
postwar financial agreements, particularly by the Bretton
Woods Agreement, as well as by American control of world
trade, which was codified by tariff agreements established
by an international conference on the matter (GATT), and
also by the establishment of an international mechanism of
monetary control (the International Monetary Fund), both
under the political domination of the United States. The
price paid for this position—especially in the Cold War cli-
mate—was the militarization of the American economy and
the related notion that the United States should assume a
protective role in the "free world." Despite the economic
effort imposed by such a policy, control of the international
market rewarded the United States Treasury with profit. Because of the surplus in the balance of trade, it was possible
both to keep armies abroad and to invest outside the United
States. The dollar continued to function as a compass to
guide the health of the world economy.

It was under such circumstances that American corporations increased their action in the periphery of the capitalist

system, as well as in European countries, by means of increased investments and expansion of their control over local economies. To this end, they invested funds and used their domestic savings primarily to purchase assets belonging to nationals. Later, the profits created by the "foreign sector" of the American economy forced it to expand continually abroad. If we add to all this the reconstruction policy carried out in Europe, we shall have an idea of the power of the American economy. In short, the United States assumed the role of bankers and stockholders in industrial and service companies, and of world policeman. In return, it offered the Western world defense against the Soviets, an industrial-technological civilization, and preservation of "basic values" (among which was the type of economy which assured the United States international predominance).

However, the end of the Cold War and several socialist successes, as well as the renewed strength of the capitalist economies in Europe and Japan (stemming in part from their refusal to defray the costs of defense against the Soviets), began to unbalance the international capitalist order. More and more was required from the Treasury, and United States administrations were led to pressure the allies for a "more responsive" and less competitive attitude. Several factors contributed to this situation. One was the very economic progress brought about by the United States through its investments; another was the more or less permanent technological revolution of the postwar decades and its dissemination and marketing, particularly by Japan and Germany (e.g., the coming of the jet, the space race, transistorization, computerization—in a word, the "communications revolution" with all of its economic consequences—as well as the growing use of synthetic materials and electronic products, etc.). There were also the increased responsibilities of the United States vis-à-vis competition from the Soviet Union, which challenged it first with Gagarin's flight and then by showing itself capable of competing in the atomic race and perhaps of surpassing the United States in conventional armaments.

The allies' response was varied. There was the Gaullist insubordination, which resulted in France's nuclear policy and in its leaving NATO, in addition to more direct consequences on an economic level, such as limitations on American penetration into the French economy, disputes concerning aircraft (the Mirage and the Concorde), and systematic attacks against the supremacy of the dollar. Since the 1960s the French have proposed that gold be substituted for the dollar as the international reserve currency. There was, on the other hand, the growing acquiescence to American pressures on the part of the British economy. Somewhere between the two, the Germans and Japanese took advantage of their strategic position in international confrontation and made concessions in political and military matters, but not in commercial ones.

Even more important, however, the very success of American companies abroad—that is, the multinationals—paradoxically caused difficulties for the American economy. Those corporations accumulated financial assets abroad, thus putting pressure on the United States Treasury, since the growth rate of the investments abroad went up faster than the export rate. By early 1970 it was becoming apparent that American expansion abroad had stimulated the other developed capitalist economies faster than it had the American national economy itself, and that the productivity and technological development of the foreign economies, paradoxically fostered by American penetration, had made them competitive.

None of this means that the American economy "has reached its limits," a static idea which helps little in an understanding of history. It does mean, however, that intercapitalist contradictions have sharpened, and that the threat both to the dollar and to the institutions set up at the end of the war to control the international economy was no longer based, during the 1970s, exclusively on General De Gaulle's policies (which preached the devaluation of the dollar and the need to reorganize the capitalist economic order). In

addition, the threat was supported by the behavior of multinational corporations, many of which had their headquarters
in the United States. The deficits of the Treasury were
matched by the financial solvency of the multinationals,
converted into "foreign" currencies: marks, yens, Swiss
francs, and French francs. Several runs on the dollar, sometimes stimulated by speculation on the part of the multinationals, but actually based on the imbalance of trade and
military expenditures, began to show that serious problems
were brewing.

Added to these structural pressures against American
economic hegemony were the growing costs of the inglorious
Vietnam war and the 1973 oil crisis, brought about not only
by OPEC but also by the fact that the oil multinationals
adjusted themselves to OPEC policies and benefited from
them more than was proportionate. As a result, the dollar
crisis became evident, and a domestic inflationary process
took hold in the United States. Important measures would
have to be taken to set things straight again.

American reaction did not take long. In 1974 Project
Independence was initiated to increase oil production and
technology; the International Energy Agency was created as
a response to OPEC, and the 1974 Trade Reform Act, with its
protectionist policies, aimed at safeguarding the position of
the United States in the world market. Unemployment, the
fight against inflation, and credit control compounded Nix-
on's and Ford's measures. Thus, at the cost of restrictions on
the Third World, of pressures on the Japanese and European
allies (who, with the exception of France, joined the "autonomist" efforts of the United States), and at the expense of
the American people, who paid the cost of "stagflation" and
unemployment, the bases were set for American Big Business
to regain international economic control. In this process the
multinational corporations and the United States government
complemented rather than fought each other. If results are
not so brilliant in the future as in the past, this will be because, in spite of everything, America has lost some of its

capacity to control the international political order, and a price will have to be paid for this. The defeats in Vietnam and Southeast Asia, recognition of China, the impossibility of intervening in Africa, side by side with a more appeasing policy toward the Arab countries, have all been the direct expression of a rebalancing of international order. Political facts like these establish the limits for reorganization of the international capitalist economy, but at the same time they are themselves conditioned by it. This picture explains the viability of the moderate and marginally autonomist policies of some peripheral countries: the international political equilibrium has been disrupted, and as a result, more room to maneuver is open to new political situations in the Third World.

It was in the context we have briefly summarized above that multinational corporations expanded in Latin America and in the rest of the world. This expansion has contributed to speculation concerning the future of capitalist economy and the role which the state plays in it. In accord with a recently proposed characterization,[1] three fundamental ways of considering the relationship between the state and the multinationals may be mentioned:

—The liberal theory, followed by those who accept the "sovereignty at bay" model proposed by Raymond Vernon. This model sees in the multinationals the nucleus of future progress and the rationalizing principle of a new world market integrated under their control, and in which the state will play a marginal role.

—The "dependence" model, which denies the balancing effect of multinationals in the redistribution of wealth and benefits on a world scale. This model emphasizes that technical progress and financial control of the results of international expansion are concentrated in a few capitalist centers,

1. See Gilpin, Robert, *U.S. Power and the Multinational Corporation: The Political Economy of Foreign Direct Investment* (New York: Basic Books, 1975).

which will go on exploiting and preserving the dependence and underdevelopment of the periphery. Despite the critical view of this model, the multinationals remain privileged actors in the world scene.[2]

—The mercantile model, which underlines the importance of the nation-state as a reorienting principle of world order, and which believes that the question of the future is not so much the disappearance of states and the preeminence of a kind of "world corporation" organized on the basis of the multinationals, but rather that it is precisely one of defining limits, conflicts, and compromises between states and multinationals, by means of the formation of regional blocks in the world market.

We believe that an approach combining the last two models offers a more adequate explanation of the role of multinational corporations in Latin America, both as to the countries where they have their headquarters and as to the host countries. We think that to consider the multinationals independently from these countries as if they were demiurges of history leads to a double reductionism: that is, it subordinates local reaction to the "logic of accumulation of multinational corporations" and therefore to "external factors," and it minimizes the importance of political factors in the development of contemporary capitalist economy, both internationally and in individual countries.

It should also be made clear that the type of linkage between industrial multinationals and national economies varies for economic reasons. The backward and forward effects that can be expected vary according to the type of goods produced (industrial, mineral, or agricultural) and according to the production techniques and the stage of consumption aimed at (industrial input, product parts for export, durable

2. It should be clear from reading this essay that the authors do not accept this formulation of the dependence thesis. Nevertheless, they recognize that this was the version generally disseminated in the United States.

consumer goods, etc.).[3] In order to evaluate the effects of incorporating peripheral economies into world production, it is further necessary to distinguish at least four situations that can create a linkage between dependent economies and market internationalization:

—"Industrial platforms" for the exportation of industrial products may be established in countries where the multinational corporations primarily seek comparative advantages, such as the use of cheap labor, and where the final product is not consumed (as in the case of Singapore or Hong Kong).

—Former enclaves of colonial production may be transformed into enclaves controlled no longer by colonialist states, but rather by imperialist corporations, as in the case of mining in Africa and the production of tropical foods.

—Parts for complex industrial products may be produced which, although not necessarily consumed in the local market, presuppose more specialized labor and relatively advanced technology in the local economy.

—Consumer or capital industrial goods may be produced under the control of multinational corporations, but aimed primarily at local markets.

There have been cases of enclave economies in Latin America that have been redefined to the extent that the world economy has become "multinationalized," for example, bauxite production in Jamaica, oil drilling in Ecuador, or banana production in Guatemala. However, the last two forms of linkage are more significant because their effects are more complex and usually occur together. The region offers few relevant examples of "industrial export platforms" controlled by multinational corporations. Exportable industrial consumer goods, such as shoes and textiles, are controlled essentially by local companies, except in the special case of

3. On this point see Hirschman, Albert, "A Generalized Linkage Aproach to Development with Special Reference to Staply" (Institute for Advanced Study, mimeo, 1976).

the cosmetics industry in Mexico. Consumer goods (automobiles, refrigerators, television sets, etc.) produced by multinationals may be exported, but in general this is due to pressures exerted by local governments wishing to solve incidental problems in their balance of payments. Even so, the bulk of durable consumer goods produced is destined for local markets.

This is why, particularly in the industrially more developed countries (Argentina, Brazil, Chile, Colombia, Peru, Venezuela, and Mexico), the issues of historical significance do not have to do with the relationship between a "consuming" bourgeoisie (such as is found in Asia or Africa) and the multinational corporations. Instead, they have to do with the relationships between local bourgeoisie, the state, and the multinationals, together with the various possible reactions to the alliances that these participants may define.

It is for this reason that in the case of the capitalistically more developed countries in the region, one must consider the form that dependence assumes when there is room for some kind of associated capitalistic development. Here the role of the state is fundamental, and it will be treated in a separate section. However, before we develop this theme, we should point out the immediate political effects brought about by the current way in which the internationalizing process of markets and production continues. It should be emphasized that if this line of analysis were followed, it would be too general (abstract) and therefore incorrect to insist solely on economic conditioning (that is, on the "logic of accumulation of multinationals") as if such conditioning (which is a point of departure for the explanation) did not depend on class struggle and, internationally, on conflicts between states. Let us consider, then, in decreasing order of abstraction, how the action of the states appears on the international stage.

Dependence and International Politics

After the failure in April 1961 of the invasion of the Bay of Pigs by Cubans armed and supported by the United States administration, and after the subsequent (and consequent)

Cuban missile crisis in October 1962, which ended with the formal agreement between Khrushchev and the Kennedy administration that there would be no new invasions on the island, certain trends in United States-Latin American relations began to take on a clearer outline.

These trends can only be interpreted in the context of the end of the Cold War and the emergence of the Soviet policy of "peaceful coexistence," the consequences of which have led to the policy of détente still in force. This policy, in turn, is linked to developments and imbalances in the technological and military race between the United States and the Soviet Union, which have had widespread repercussions on the international economy and the balance of power as a whole. It is also linked, in a special way, to the dispute between the United States and the European Common Market (France in particular) on the one hand, and between the Soviet Union and China on the other. At the same time, as was mentioned in the previous section, the international capitalist economy was entering a phase of competition and new polarization around dynamic centers that previously had been considered mere extensions of the American economy: Japan and Western Europe, and in the latter, France and Germany in particular.

In this context, the turning point may have been the signing of the Test Ban Treaty in August 1963 by the Soviet Union, the United States, and England, and the clear refusal of China and France to support it. The French opposition was based on a strategy aimed at guaranteeing its ability to strike "in all directions." From that point, the concept of a policy of unconditional allies lost force in the Western bloc. So as not to leave it to the Russians and Americans to decide whether French territory would be the object of their bargaining or agreements, De Gaulle created an independent military industrial system. By doing so he was able not only to bring down the domestic costs of decolonization—by replacing the old colonial economic interests with a financial industrial economy organized around the creation of an advanced technology and war industry—but also to endow

France with an atomic "force de frappe" capable of launching attacks—and therefore of retaliating—independently of Soviet-American will.

The consequences of Chinese opposition were far greater. From 1963 on it became apparent that the world political chessboard was no longer divided into two blocs, but into at least three, and that there were important divisions among the allies in each of the rival blocs. Such divisions led to the dismissal of any notion that the world might be divided in half between the Soviets and the Americans by a new Treaty of Tordesillas, as it were.[4]

Despite these difficulties, the military, economic, and technological superiority of the United States and the Soviet Union is such that in their areas of direct influence, especially after détente and the SALT negotiations, the Kissinger-Brezhnev policy seeks to freeze the developments and rebelliousness which "peaceful coexistence" might encourage in the peripheral countries. The presence of China, added to the economic recession and the American defeat in Vietnam (which are intrinsically linked to successive crises of the dollar, caused by the war costs and the changes in world structure already mentioned, as well as by the struggles against American hegemony), has made it difficult, however, to reach that goal. United States recognition of China in 1972, the growing difficulties of reaching an agreement between the Soviets and the Chinese, China's public demonstration of atomic capability, all have been highly unsettling factors for the dream of a Soviet-American peace.

The still unsolved problem of redefining the world political order in such a way as to replace the bipolarization of the Cold War period has been made difficult by Kissinger's desire for an "enlightened bipolarization." The Soviet Union might, however reticently, support this game, and show that

4. Reference is to the fifteenth-century treaty whereby Portugal and Spain divided the territories to be discovered.

it also has an enlightened face by granting emigration visas and by a relative tolerance of non-aligned friends in its periphery. However, China's presence and the reopening of several diplomatic missions in Western Europe, as well as the anticolonial struggle and Third World struggles in general, complicate things and make it difficult for the world order to depend steadily on the Washington–Moscow red telephone connection.

The consequences of the end of the Cold War and the crisis in the world political order, added to the more recent consequences of recession and especially the OPEC reaction, were felt somewwhat late in Latin America. Beginning in the 1970s, however, they began to weigh heavily on the foreign policy of the area as well as on the behavior of the great powers.

In the first place, after the Soviet-American agreement on Cuba (and here it should be emphasized that, at first sight, the military victory in the Bay of Pigs invasion was Cuban, not Soviet), it took the ministries of foreign affairs on the continent a decade to recognize that Cuban socialism will not be removed through external pressures. The policy of blockade and sabotage against Cuba began to give way to another, which had always been that of Mexico: a policy of distant tolerance on the part of the majority of the countries that have recognized Cuba diplomatically, and in the case of some governments, such as Peru, one of discreetly supporting the Cubans.

The policy of détente has led the United States to maintain a position of disdainful covert interference with respect to Latin America. Two qualifications, however, are necessary.

1. The tolerance which the State Department shows publicly in cases of deviance from the canons of unconditional submission to American interests is counterbalanced by the veiled but always effective support which American special forces lend to local rightist groups organized to "destabilize" governments that might take steps toward more radical forms of nationalism or socialism.

2. The State Department and the military branches of the United States administration show much more rigidity with regard to changes in Central America and particularly in the Caribbean. In this area, United States policy is susceptible to geo-political considerations because of interests that are perceived and defined as strategic for American military defense and that are supported by the existence of colonial enclaves, such as the Panama Canal, Puerto Rico, and Guantánamo. Even though such considerations are anachronistic from a strictly military viewpoint, they find political and economic support among reactionary circles in the United States. Even purely national-reformist tendencies (such as those which took shape in Santo Domingo in 1965) are perceived as an intolerable challenge. An exception to this rigidity has been the relative tolerance shown by the United States to the renegotiation of the status of the Panama Canal, where it faces a nationalist and moderately reformist military government. Even in this case, however, the reaction of domestic political interests has been very strong in the United States.

The counterpart of this increased flexibility on the part of the United States has been the discreet withdrawal of Cuba from the politics of the region. This is not so much a consequence of any objective conclusion drawn from the Soviet-American agreements (for guerrilla action and Cuban support to it did not stop after 1962, and even increased until at least 1970); it is rather the result of the failure, which will be mentioned below, of guerrilla tactics and of Cuban support to revolutionary movements in Venezuela, Guatemala, and Bolivia.

Under such circumstances, certain nationalist-reformist experiments of some scope, such as those in Peru, have been assimilated by American policy without major resistance. Peru's decision to resist external intervention, the logistic difficulties of a military expedition outside the Caribbean, added to the hard lesson of Vietnam, were probably sufficient to discourage greater rigidity on the part of the United States in the negotiations. The Peruvian leaders carried out some important changes, but these were limited, in general, to 25 percent of the less impoverished population; this, plus the fact that they have implemented investment agreements considered practicable for the multinational corporations, has probably helped to weaken the temptation of applying to Peru measures based on the Hickenlooper amendment as well as to discourage a more consistent boycott against that country by the international financing centers. However, we should not minimize the Peruvian regime's performance, aimed at implementing measures in terms of a program and certain proposed goals which, although inescapable, had not been worked out or effected by previous regimes. The lack of viable political alternatives that might have been implemented by the internal opposition and the moderate nature of Peruvian policies would have reduced the effectiveness of foreign intervention had it been attempted.[5]

As is well known, external action was very different in the Chilean experiment. In this case, the internal conditions existed for "foreign aid" to destabilizing groups to be effective, and the international economic siege was implemented quickly and efficiently.

There is no need for detailed comment on the official American aid to repressive regimes in the region and for the training of anti-guerrilla groups. However, it would be inadequate to limit the analysis of United States action in Latin America to its power of veto and coercion. Equally important is the support given by the United States to certain policies. The most recent American administrations have considered Latin America an area of marginal interest and have carried on a policy that has replaced the more active goals of the Alliance for Progress in the Kennedy period with the restrictive policies mentioned above. The active encouragement

5. On the Peruvian situation and the themes mentioned here in particular, see Lowenthal, Abraham F., "Peru's Ambiguous Revolution," especially p. 13, in Lowenthal, A., ed., *The Peruvian Experiment* (Princeton: Princeton University Press, 1975).

given to those repressive military regimes capable of blocking structural changes, and the unrestricted support of economic policies designed to make capitalist growth viable in under-developed countries (especially in the case of Brazil), consti-tute the other constant in the relations between the United States and Latin America.

We do not believe that processes such as the recent growth of an associate-dependent-capitalist economy in Bra-zil, or the continuing growth of the Mexican economy, can be explained through "foreign aid." This would be to ignore specific local conditions, for other countries, such as Chile and Uruguay, have received foreign aid without reaping the desired fruits of economic growth. But it is undeniable that, as a matter of policy, administrations in the United States have given unrestricted support during the last ten years to any government, military, repressive, or authoritarian as it might be, that showed an interest in fostering the alliance between the local states and the interests of the multinational corporations. In this respect, in spite of speculation about the growing autonomy of those corporations from the United States, there has been, in Latin America at least, a concur-rence of interests and policies between Big Business and American administrations. It may be argued that the interests of some companies were not sufficiently defended at crucial moments by the American government in Peru or in Chile. It is true that the American state has not equated the interests of the United States as a nation with those of one corporation or another, and it is also true that given the political goals of the United States in Latin America, as well as the current world situation, it would be unrealistic to expect an invasion in response to each expropriation; however, as a matter of general policy, the United States administrations have tried to guarantee the maximal success of market internationaliza-tion with a minimum of political friction.

It must be recognized that, considering its goals and without passing judgment on the means employed ("desta-bilization," "dirty conspiracy," support of repressive govern-ments, etc.), the main objectives of American policy in the region have been attained. The cost of this success may be measured by the fact that there were few situations in Latin America in which regimes guaranteeing some public freedom survived, and even fewer regimes that constantly tried to support development policies beneficial to the welfare of the majority. In general, distant goals for the welfare of all are proposed, and in the meantime, not only the freedom but also the material well-being of the national majority is sacrificed, in spite of economic performances that are impressive for those who benefit from them.

To conclude this section, several policies of reaction against the international order which have been attempted in Latin America should be mentioned. In this regard, it might be useful to point out that there have been four basic forms of reaction to the international order in Latin America:

1. A number of countries have not only kept a low profile but have also remained close to the norms of a submissive acceptance of American goals (sometimes because of an absence of any real alternatives) in the reorganization of the international order. The voting record of countries like Paraguay, Nicaragua, or Haiti at the United Nations offers concrete examples of the extent to which national states can be limited by a situation of pervasive dependence. Even in a rebellious U.N., many Latin American countries have failed to take part in the movement labeled "the dictatorship of the majority" by the United States representative when it began to oppose American goals.

2. Socialist countries like Cuba, or those which at certain moments had governments with socialist aspirations, like Chile, or nationalist-reformist aspirations, like Peru or Guyana, have tried to strengthen their policies of solidarity with the Third World and of support to the reorganization of the economic order by the formation of cartels such as OPEC, OCIPEC (copper), bauxite, and so forth.[6] Their capacity to

6. Obviously, we cannot go into details here. For an examination of advances in the attempts at economic defense on the part of producers of raw materials, see Vaitsos, Constantine V., "Power,

implement such policies was obviously restricted, given the precariousness of local governments and the lack of a real base of economic interests in some of the proposed experiments (with the exception of oil).

3. Attempts to eliminate or decrease dependence were made by the countries that formed the Andean Pact and by those that proposed the creation of an Economic Office for Latin America (SELA), without United States participation and with the objective of self-reliance. In the case of the Andean Pact, Bolivia, Chile, Peru, Ecuador, Colombia, and Venezuela, following Peru's initiative, negotiated a treaty on foreign investments, which gives the national states some power to control the multinationals, and which tries to develop the concept of subregional integrated markets as a response to the limitations of local markets. In the case of SELA, Mexico and Venezuela (the latter motivated by the availability of exchange currency as a result of the oil boom) led in an articulation of embassies, with the unenthusiastic support of Brazil, to encourage the proposal of policies of Latin American interest and scope. The Venezuelan government opened credit lines for several Caribbean and Central American countries to compensate for difficulties in the balance of payments and to create assistance funds. In an effort to dispel apprehensions about the possibility of a "pre-imperialist" type of action, the countries leading SELA have negotiated agreements generally favorable to the countries that participate in them.

4. Finally, some Latin American countries, particularly Brazil, Mexico, and Venezuela, besides Cuba, seem to concentrate their efforts on developing a foreign policy on a world level. Venezuela, stimulated by OPEC, has become

---

Knowledge and Development Policy: Relations Between Transnational Enterprises and Developing Countries," in Hellenir, G. K., ed., *A World Divided: The Less Developed Country in the International Economy* (Cambridge: Cambridge University Press, 1973).

active not only in SELA but also in international meetings, where it has defined itself within a political range that goes beyond the relationship of economic subordination of a country that depends upon its oil exports to the United States. Mexico has tried to implement Third World policies, keeping up a strong autonomist rhetoric, even though it has maintained, if not expanded, its structural economic dependence upon the United States. Its international position in Latin America has been marked by its strong diplomatic support for the Chilean socialist experiment as well as by the continuation of its traditional policy of limited but permanent contact with Cuba.

In this context, Brazil shows some less-expected facets, given its current economic model and its explicit policy of support for the United States since 1964. The consequences of the breakdown of world bipolarity and of the fact that military confrontation between the United States and the Soviet Union is not expected, as well as of the presence of China on the world scene, have led the Brazilian governments since 1968 to define an international policy that keeps its distance from American foreign policy on some important points: Brazil did not sign the Atomic Agreement and later established its own agreement with Germany for the building of atomic reactors and the transfer of nuclear technology; like other Latin American countries, it unilaterally declared its sovereignty over territorial waters up to two hundred miles; pressured by the need to import oil, it has signed agreements with the Arab countries, and more recently, in 1974, it recognized the MPLA government in Angola, a country with which Brazilian governments have been trying for years to negotiate economic agreements.

It should be emphasized that the more significant changes in the foreign policy of Latin America would be unthinkable but for the prevailing conditions in the world scene, which have disrupted the previous balance and opened opportunities for new national policies. These, of course, can only have strength and credibility abroad when the domestic political order is relatively stable; for this reason Argentina, the Latin American country which in the past was most active internationally, has had a lessened role in recent years.

It is also evident that the emergence of Latin American countries trying to exercise power at the international level poses questions with regard to the areas of regional influence. Without going into the details of this controversial question, we should clarify the fact that neither Mexico nor Venezuela nor Brazil—three of the most active countries in international politics—has limited its action to Latin America. They seem to aim at establishing a place for themselves in the international political order, particularly in the case of Brazil, which has intensified not only its political but basically its economic relations with Germany, Japan, and Africa. This observation does not diminish the impact which the more active presence of economic and political interests of these countries may have upon neighboring nations. The expressed concern of Trinidad or the Guianas about Venezuela, or of Central American countries about Mexico, or the action of Brazil in Paraguay, in Bolivia, and even in Uruguay have shown this. However, it seems premature to speak of sub-imperialism, as if the multinationals were behind the foreign policy of these countries in a direct way, or as if their international political action were the expression of some supposed need to export capital or consumer goods caused by limitations of its domestic market. There are indeed relationships between economic interests and foreign policies, and there is interference by some Latin American states in other countries in the area; however, the role of the state in the economy and in the articulation of economic and political interests in those countries must be analyzed more carefully, as we shall see below, before we can qualify those interventions as the result of sub-imperialism. Not always and not necessarily do Latin American embassies respond only to the interests and pressures of the United States or the multinationals. There are other interests—and other passions—which lead some states in the periphery to act in search of a place among the powerful nations. Some of these interests and these passions (or ideologies), as well as their limitations, will be pointed out below in the discussion of the relationships between the local states and the economic order.

Capitalist Development and the State: Bases and Alternatives

The more developed countries of Latin America are attempting to define foreign policy objectives that take advantage of contradictions in the international order and allow these countries some independent policy-making. But these countries remain dependent and assure an internal social order favorable to capitalist interests and consequently fail to challenge one of the basic objectives of American foreign policy. Multinational enterprises continue to receive support from the foreign policies of their countries of origin, as well as from local states.

How can these contradictory forces act together? It is through contradictions that the historical process unfolds. Dependent development occurs through frictions, accords, and alliances between the state and business enterprises. But this type of development also occurs because both the state and business enterprises pursue policies that form markets based on the concentration of incomes and on the social exclusion of majorities. These processes demand a basic unity between these two historical actors as they confront popular opposition, which may be activated when nationalist or socialist movements question the existing social order. So, the conflicts between the state and Big Business are not as antagonistic as the contradictions between dominant classes and people.

Within the last ten years, the strengthening of the state and the penetration of multinational corporations occurred within the context of a new set of class relations. On one hand, attempts were made to break (sometimes radically) with the global situation of dependency, with the aim of transforming society in the direction of socialism. On the other hand, dominant classes were reordered, with emphasis placed on the repressive role of the state and on the simultaneous transformation of the state into a tool for the fortification of the capitalist economic order.

The exhaustion of the prior populism and the aggravation of class tensions gave rise to various political attempts to break with the prevailing style of development. In one form or another, during the past decade, the politics of Latin American popular forces were profoundly marked by the presence of the Cuban revolution. The shadow of Guevara's deeds and the quasi-substitution of the process of mass politics by the military actions of guerrilla groups (though this was not implicit in their theory) considerably polarized Latin American revolutionary movements. These attempts failed nearly everywhere, the only exception of consequence being the case of Argentina, where the two principal guerrilla currents were not completely dissociated from the remaining socio-political movements. Though not constituting a real political power alternative, the guerrillas of Argentina exert a certain veto capacity, conditioning other political movements and attempts at reformulating class alliances.

Attempts at radical rupture with the capitalist-developmentalist path were not limited to the politics of the guerrilla. The Chilean popular unity of the Allende period, as one case, and the Peruvian military reformism, as another, were reactions based on broader popular forces to development that is tied to international capitalist-oligopolistic expansion. In both cases the state was viewed not as a "bourgeois institution" to be destroyed, but as the lever for a possible total transformation of society, on condition that its control remain in the hands of popular forces.

Both the battle between classes and the basic dependency relationship find in the state a natural crossroads. The contradiction of a state that constitutes a nation without being sovereign is the nucleus of the subject matter of dependency. Our rereading the history has proceeded throughout the book toward specifying the fundamental historical actors: classes and groups defined within specific forms of production. Now, after ten years of reasonable rates of economic growth, the expansion of global commerce, the industrialization of important segments of the periphery of the capitalist world, and the strengthening of the state productive sector, the problem unfolds in a more complex manner. *Strictu sensu,* the capacity for action of various Latin American states has increased. In this sense, one might consider that they are "less dependent." Our concern is not, however, to measure degrees of dependency in these terms—which fail to ask, "less for whom? for which classes and groups?" Which classes have become more sovereign? Which alliances and class interests within each country and at the international level lead the historical process of economic development?

If the state has expanded and fortified itself, it has done so as the expression of a class situation which has incorporated both threats of rupture with the predominant pattern of capitalist development, as we have said, and policies of the dominant classes favorable to the rapid growth of the corporate system, to alliances between the state and business enterprises, and to the establishment of interconnections, at the level of the state productive system, between "public" and multinational enterprises. To accomplish this, the state has assumed an increasingly repressive character, and dominant classes in a majority of countries have proposed policies increasingly removed from popular interest. They have rendered viable a "peripheral" capitalist development, adopting a growth model based on replication—almost in caricature of the consumption styles and industrialization patterns of the central capitalist countries. The tendencies indicated in chapter six developed with increasing velocity, achieving successes for that style of development (the "Brazilian miracle" and the type of growth that occurred in Mexico until 1970, are notable examples of the trend). Given conditions in Latin America, this process, while producing economic

growth, urbanization, and wealth, has redefined without eliminating, or else in certain cases has aggravated the existential,
social, and economic problems of a majority of the population. This majority has come to be looked upon as a resource
for the accumulation of capital more than as the effective potential for the creation of a society modeled on its own interests.

Under these conditions, the state and the nation have
become separated: all that is authentically popular, even if
lacking the character of specific class demands, has come
under suspicion, is considered subversive, and encounters a
repressive response. In this vein, even problems which Western capitalist democracies confront and absorb, like the discussion of income distribution, minority movements (blacks,
Indians, migrants, etc.), feminist or youth demands (not to
mention the freedom of syndical and political organization),
appear threatening to the existing order. From the perspective of the dominant classes, the nation has become increasingly confused with the state, and the latter in turn has
identified its interests with theirs, resulting in the confusion
of the public interest with the defense of the business enterprise system.

Local dominant groups in Latin America responded to
the external influences on economic growth and to the need
to guard against attempts to transform the prevailing order,
with an amalgam between a repressive state (often under
corporate military control) and an entrepreneurial state.
What lends dynamism to this form of state, and what characterizes its movement, is *not* the bureaucratic aspect it may
have assumed in some countries (Peru, Mexico, Brazil, Chile,
among the most characteristic cases), but rather its *entrepreneurial* aspect, which leads it to ally itself, in production,
with the multinational corporation. Somehow, the state has
become a strategic element, functioning as a hinge that permits the opening of the portals through which capitalism
passes into industrializing peripheral economies.

A state which expanded the public sector *at the same
time* that it intensified relations between the latter and the

multinational corporations began to develop with the accords on the "Chileanization" of copper proposed by the government of Frei. The proposal was uncommon in the statist tradition of Latin America: the connection with foreign enterprises would be made through their association, not with the local bourgeoisie, but with public enterprises created by the state, which come to function as *corporations.*

The generalization of this model, in Brazil, in Mexico, in Peru, in Venezuela, for example, transferred the conflicts *among associates* to a more directly political sphere. In addition, it married foreign interests with the local bourgeoisie, and in certain countries, with the interests of local states insofar as they were direct agents of production, as occurred in Brazil, in Mexico, and to a lesser extent in Venezuela. The consequences of this process are enormous and are far from having been exhausted by historical practice or by analysis. The character of this state-as-entrepreneur and of the state associated economically with imperialist forces without being a politically associated state has lent to the contemporary form of the state a significance different from that which it had until mid-1950.

What is novel is the expansion of the state's direct productive investment in capitalistically profitable sectors. While state investments in these sectors originally came about with resources obtained through taxes and duties, they subsequently reproduced and expanded through the *profits* generated by the state enterprises (petrochemicals, mining, direct consumer goods, etc.). In countries like Brazil, Chile, Colombia, Peru, Mexico, and Venezuela, the public sector contributes more than 50 percent to the annual formation of capital, with the remainder contributed by private national and foreign enterprises. Of this total, in a majority of these countries, the *state enterprises* (as an individual portion of public expenditure) constitute more than half of the investment of the public sector. In Brazil, in 1975, this figure exceeded 30 percent of the total investment (public and private). Also in Brazil, the only two local enterprises which,

by the scope of their action, could hope to qualify as multinationals (aside from the Itaipu hydroelectric corporation)
are state enterprises: the Vale do Rio Doce and Petrobras.
Counted among the largest enterprises operating in Brazil,
in terms of assets and the value of production or trade (and
leaving foreign enterprises aside), are not the enterprises
controlled by local private capital, but rather those of the
state. In 1975, fifty-six of the one hundred largest Brazilian
enterprises were state owned.[7]

The role of bureaucracies and of technocrats is considerable in practically all of the industrialized countries of Latin
America. In a penetrating essay on this subject,[8] Guillermo
O'Donnell attempts to show the nature of this form of
regime and the conditions under which it emerges. He points
out that regimes of this type established themselves in the
region as the response of local dominant classes to the challenge presented by the mobilization and popular pressure
generated by the collapse of previous political orders (either
populist or traditionally authoritarian). He adduces further
that this collapse occurred when economic difficulties that
followed the import-substitution stage of industrialization
created an inflationary situation and led the economy into
an impasse. Its solution required, aside from stability to
ensure economic predictability, additional capital flows and
greater entrepreneurial centralization in order to proceed
along an oligopolistic route toward the continuation of the
process of accumulation and toward the development of productive forces. O'Donnell concludes that, for all of these
reasons, there exists a relationship of "mutual indispensibility" between bureaucratic-authoritarian states and international capital (which needs to penetrate local economies

7. It should be made clear that despite the importance of the
role of the state productive sector in the Brazilian economy, foreign
enterprises control between 40 and 50 percent of the large groups,
according to measures of fixed assets, liquid assets, employment,
and invoicing.

8. O'Donnell, Guillermo, "Reflexiones sobre las tendencias
generales de cambio en el Estado burocratico autoritario" (Buenos
Aires, CEDES, 1975).

and which possesses the technological and financial requisites to undertake the "deepening of development").

The lack of local private investment potential, the political need to prevent multinational corporations from single-handedly appropriating the most strategic sectors of the economy and their most dynamic branches, and even, at times, the nonexistence of international capital flows to attend to the investment needs of peripheral countries during any given period (since multinationals act on a global scale, aiming at maximizing results and not toward the continuity of local development), has led local states, despite the capitalist ideology they defend, to expand their functions and thereby to create a national basis from which to bargain with the multinationals. In this process, neither the decisions of the state nor the pressure from multinationals excludes local enterprises from the game. But in practice these local enterprises continue to lag behind the principal agents of transformation: the multinationals and the state. By the very force of expansion, new investment prospects do at times open up for segments of the local bourgeois sectors. Some of these return to the political-economic offensive, often allying themselves with the multinational enterprises in the "anti-statist" struggle.

This summary of contemporary development lies within what we perceived as possible ten years ago. The role of the state and how it supports itself in industrialized-peripheral countries has become more clear, however.

If it seems necessary for the state in a dependent-capitalist country to become bureaucratic if expansion is to be viable, then the risk is run of relying on economic reductionism, which cannot take account of historical processes.[9] For example, it may be true that Argentina's General Onganía

9. We are not referring here to O'Donnell's analyses. There exists in these (especially in "Notas para uma explicação histórico-comparativa" [Notes for an histórico-comparative analysis], mimeo) a vivid effort to demonstrate that the "mutual indispensibility" between oligopolistic accumulation and bureaucratic-authoritarian regimes passes through the sieve of class struggles and through the accidents of history.

had a corporativist political plan, which tended to bureau-
cratize the state apparatus and implement repressive policies.
Nonetheless, the Cordobazo—a mass rebellion—together
with the force of the labor movement, Peronism, and the
enunciations of guerrilleros and revolutionaries, prevented
Onganía's plan from working. President Lanusse later proposed a pact with Peronism, which aimed at preventing an
alliance between revolutionary movements and the Peronist
masses, which would have been dangerous to the capitalist
order. After Perón's death, the inability of a government
controlled by a mass bureaucratic party to thwart the revolutionary challenge led to the coup of General Videla. Was this
coup an implementation of a bureaucratic-authoritarian regime based on the dynamism of public enterprise? Not necessarily. In the Argentinian case, social classes and the private
economy constitute a force which until now has escaped the
political-corporativist control of the state (though the labor
movement and labor unions contain corporativist ties). Corporativist projects expire under syndical pressures and under
the economic pressures of export sectors when these demand
free market prices (one of General Videla's first acts was to
remove the commercialization of meat from state control). In
the Argentinian case, in moments of advancing revolutionary
pressures, the state has assumed a repressive-military form,
without having produced until now a stable bureaucratic-
authoritarian regime.[10]

In Venezuela and Colombia, especially in the former,
the state is promoting ties between multinational enterprises
and the public sector to strengthen the public sector, but
without a bureaucratic-authoritarian regime. To be sure, it

10. On the contradictions in the recent evolution of the economy
and politics of Argentina, consult O'Donnell's text, referred to
above. The alliance between part of the local bourgeoisie and the
popular-worker movement constitutes, for that author, a defensive
alliance whose limits emerge clearly when the cyclical oscillations
of the economy lead agro-exporting sectors to demand corrections
in the economic policies proposed by this alliance.

represses the challenge of "outlaws," as does every dominant order. But it does not exclude party politics, the representation of interests, and some public freedoms. These are examples of a pact of domination favorable to big business in a situation of class conflict in which a formally democratic regime does not give way to the emergence of more repressive forms of political organization.

The Argentinian example demonstrates the "open process" of history. A simple "structural" analysis, demonstrating the contradictions between social forces and the drawbacks of the process of accumulation with its cycles and crises is insufficient to explain the concrete course of political events. Nor does it suffice to point out the affinities and battles among dominant classes and the plans for political institutionalization which they support. It is even insufficient to view the political behavior of ruling classes in terms of reaction to a popular challenge. Popular reaction, under the guerrilla form, as we saw in Argentina, was capable of conditioning and of vetoing but not of transforming the political structure. There have been no viable alliances capable of imposing a form of state which could recover not only the aspiration to sovereignty but the primacy of the popular interest. The incapacity for hegemony of popular groups adds to the repressive capacity of dominant classes the fatal ingredient that leads to a policy of advance and retreat within the iron circle of prevailing structures.

In Brazil and in Peru, the fortification of a formally bureaucratic-authoritarian order can be seen more clearly. The state in Brazil does not adopt, as an ideology, the authoritarianism which it practices. Thus the regime is guided by a duality of principles: the constitutional order that anticipates, for example, elections; and the institutional acts that transform the military president into de facto dictator, as long as the political order is perceived to be threatened, according to criteria determined by the organs of military security. Despite these instruments of discretion, the failure to explicitly recognize the validity of an authoritarian order leads the regime into the exercise of electoral practices which at times jeopardize authoritarianism. The government dismantles the very "legal" order it created, by impeding the rotation in power of the two parties, by eliminating elected deputies, by going against the "democratic ideal."

In Peru, where the regime is clearly nonparticipatory, the qualifying phrase "bureaucratic authoritarian" is more immediately applicable: public enterprise and the state as a bureaucratic organization both expand while remaining under the control of the military corporation. Meanwhile, social and economic policy in Peru, while not revolutionary, is not income-concentrating, in comparison with what occurs when the multinationals and the private sector of the local economy direct the process of accumulation. In addition, political control does not assume traits that are abusive of human rights, as occurs in Chile and in Brazil or Argentina.

The contradiction between the state as the agent of capitalist enterprise, and the nation as something that is essentially popular, follows a movement that is not only different but *opposite,* in the recent history of Peru and Brazil. Though the Peruvian state may be bureaucratic-authoritarian, its policies are oriented toward the incorporation of the masses, or at least toward the partial consideration of peasant and popular interests. These objectives may have been frustrated and difficult to secure within a policy that stifled the spontaneity of popular reaction, congealed political parties, and harbored seeds of military-bureaucratism. However, its ideology and what it has done to reorganize the socio-economic order distinguish the Peruvian state from that of the bureaucratic-authoritarian state of Brazil.

Political regimes vary, as does the relation of bureaucratic-authoritarianism to the social bases of the state (viewed as a pact of domination). Nevertheless, the current form of dependency and the crucial role performed in it by multinational enterprises and by the state productive sector are no accident. It is necessary to draw a distinction between the state, as a basic part of domination (and not as the expression of a "social contract") which unites dominant classes in the exercise of domination over the rest of society, and the variable forms assumed by political *regimes*. The state expresses a situation of domination, reflects the interests of dominant classes, and expresses their capacity to impose themselves on subordinate classes. At the same time this discriminatory relationship (the domination of one part over the rest) must appear to the national consciousness to be the expression of a general interest. Consequently, the state constitutes a relationship of domination incorporating *an ideology* that masks that partiality. This process is not a simple distortion: it must also mirror, in some way, the generality it wishes to represent. Hence, even the most openly classist and repressive states use a language and propose policies (generally nonviable) that purport to reflect the "general interest."

So, the state expresses the imposition of one class or alliance of classes over others. But while it serves those interests on which it bases itself, the state proposes measures that lend verisimilitude to the "generality of interests" which it must assume to exist (people, equality, nation). In addition to expressing a relationship like this at this level, the state is also a bureaucratic-regulative organization and, in the case of modern states, becomes even a productive economic organization.

To summarize, any state, through bureaucratic and productive organizations, expresses a relationship of class domination (and consequently has social bases), assumes an ideology as if in the common interest, develops and implements policies that respond to the fundamental pact of domination, but also claims to attend to the aspirations of dominated groups. Officials of the state (notably in the judicial sector) have to adopt both an ideology of equality and generality ("all citizens are equal before the law") and a practice in which dominant interests impose themselves.

In the industrialized countries of Latin America which

we are considering, the state embodies an alliance between the interests of the internationalized sector of the bourgeoisie and those of public and entrepreneurial bureaucracies. The local bourgeoisie links itself to these sectors. In part, the state in dependent capitalism generates its own social base, since its productive function is to assure capital accumulation, and since in performing this function, it creates a sector of public entrepreneurs. At times this stratum is called the "state bourgeoisie," to emphasize that these social agents are not simple bureaucrats nor do they simply implement the "public good." They function, sociologically, as the "officeholders of capital." For they support the accumulation of capital in the state enterprises. Both the accumulation of capital by public enterprises and the placing of all of the national wealth (mineral ore, impounded taxes, lands, roadways, etc.) at the disposal of private capital are fundamental requirements for the advancement of associated-dependent capitalism.

The state extends a bureaucracy and bases itself on a civil and military technocracy. The latter carries out the interests that are expressed by the state. Certainly, an inversion of this relationship can occur. The actors may occupy prominent positions on the political scene. The military bureaucracy may predominate in the control of the state. But in the end, long-term policies must be compatible with the social bases of the state. In the realization of policies of accumulation and development, though the bureaucratic framework may be in the hands of a technocratic-bureaucracy or a corporative military (together or separately), the nature of the dominant state relationship develops through the strengthening of the alliance between the local entrepreneurial sector, associated with the multinational foreign enterprises, and the state productive sector.

The same fundamental alliance which constitutes a dependent industrial capitalist state may organize itself institutionally within a context of authoritarianism, restricted democracy, or totalitarianism. There is little credibility in its structural compatibility with substantive forms of mass-democracy, populism, or even traditional caudillo (bossist) authoritarianism, since in these regimes the requisite policies leading to the expansion of industrial dependent capitalism become difficult to implement, because of the masses' interests in economic redistribution and political participation.

Not that Venezuela, Colombia, and Argentina will *necessarily* have to adapt themselves to the Brazilian or Peruvian military-bureaucratic-authoritarian model. These last two regimes are themselves quite different, both in the nature of their policies and in the nature of their respective social bases. The bureaucratic-authoritarian *form* of a regime like that of Brazil is not the *only* one capable of adapting to the "present stage" of capital accumulation. Economic reductionism in this case would fail to consider the changes that might occur from government to government (with, we repeat, the basic state pact maintained). There are many factors that function as sources of dynamism in history: (1) circumstantial factors such as explosions of collective protest (the 1974 Brazilian elections provide an example different from the Cordobazo, because the correlation of forces differs in the two countries); (2) struggles within dominant sectors; (3) the emergence of objective economic challenges (recessions, soaring inflation, a "new stage" of import substitution in the capital goods sector, for example); (4) the ability of the governing group to resolve problems and the opposition's ability to debate them, and so forth. Not all changes are always possible, to be sure, nor do political forces capable of taking advantage of opportunities for transformation always exist. But even in bureaucratic-authoritarian regimes, and even with the persistence of the alliance that underlies the state, there is room for regime-types to vary historically. What is at issue is not just a "mere change in form." The differences between a torturing autocratic regime and a "restricted democracy" arise out of the very possibilities for struggles among classes, and they in turn influence the historical opportunities of the dependent capitalist-industrial state.

A basic problem exists, posed by the present moment and by Latin American situations of dependency: the very penetration of multinationals requires a state that is capable of furnishing the multinationals with the resources for accumulation. So national wealth is necessary for foreign private accumulation. But this process is contradictory: for this to work, the state must fortify itself and expand its functions at both the administrative and the economic levels, in this way increasing its prospects for sovereignity. Faced with the political challenges of dominated classes to radically reorder society, this entrepreneurial-regulative state militarizes itself, becoming even stronger and more autocratic. At this point the relative loosening of ties between the state and its *social base* may occur, which the economically ruling classes may perceive as a risk of "Bonapartization" of the state. The spectrum of this perceived risk ranges from the emergency of a new Perón to a "mythical Peruvianism" that would lead the armed forces to ally with the people. In the process of exercising sovereignty and equipping the state with entrepreneurial skills, which allow both international and local accumulation, the entrepreneurial-repressive state *dissociates* itself from the nation. *This* is the specific political contradiction in the current form of Latin American dependent development.

There may have been a redefinition of the "forms of dependency," in certain Latin American countries there may be "less dependency," and the state in these countries may be capable of exercising a greater degree of sovereignty. But for us, what is at issue is the nature of class conflicts and alliances which the dependency situation encompasses.

As we stated previously, the political struggle revolving around the state shows what is essential in this form of dependency: the style of development of the possibility of alternatives depends upon the resolution of this question of the state. In the Chilean Popular Unity, in Peru, and in the Popular Assembly of the Torres period in Bolivia, popular forces or forces with popular intentions momentarily assumed control of the state. We find, in these cases, ambiguity about what constitutes the "popular" and unanimity regarding *national* demands. The fundamental challenge of the present moment in Latin American social development consists in linking these two aspects of radical political movements, the popular and the national, and in getting to the bottom of the opposition between the popular and the proletarian. What is specific to the Latin American situation of dependency is the difficulty in conceiving of a political passage to socialism by a strictly proletarian route, given the structural conditions of industrial capitalism in the periphery. So, alliances between popular movements, national-popular demands, and properly working-class struggles are required to enforce new paths in society.

These questions, however, are not posed today as they were during the populist period. The advance of mass industrial society, urbanization, the revolution in communication, even the situations of dependent-*development* themselves, pose the political question of popular participation in such a way as to *exclude manipulative links with dominant classes through the state* as an option. Such links were the basis of populism's policy. The internationalization of production and of the market have advanced, and the state productive sector has expressed itself in capitalist form. For the ruling groups, the nation is embodied in the state as the stimulus for an enterprise economy. But, at the same time, for dominated classes, the paternalism of the traditional Latin American state (in both the oligarchical and populist versions) has been broken. Although politically frustrated, the guerrilla movements did serve the function of disrupting this paternalism and putting an end to manipulative types of alliance which once tied the people to the state in the name of the nation.

The practical issues that will permit development of an alternative type of state involve, first, knowing which course "substantive democratization" must take to affirm what is

essential in the national and the popular and free from the
rancidity of bureaucratization and authoritarianism, and
second, knowing how to balance the need for organization
and the vitality of spontaneous mass behavior. As in any case
of social transformation, such questions go beyond analysis
and anchor themselves in values: they are projected into the
future to assist in the practical escape from a situation that
reinforces the prevailing exploitative order. It is not within
the boundaries of this book to pursue these questions. It is
barely within those boundaries to point out, as we have,
that social practice in Latin America has already begun to
deal with these questions (even if in experiences that failed).

Researchers have directed their attention to ideology and
corporativist forms in Latin America.[11] It appears to us that
the fusion between enterprise and the state, both of them
based on bureaucracies, and the role of armies in Latin American regimes, underscore the corporativist ties between the
state and society.[12] During certain periods of political life, the
relationship between civil society and the state seems to dis-
pense with the mediation of parties: classes just appropriate
segments of the state apparatus to defend their interests.
Sometimes connections are formed through "bureaucratic
rings," which are organized around high officials (cabinet
ministers, generals, etc.) and which articulate the immediate
interests of enterprises, government bureaus, the press, sometimes unions, repressive groups, and so forth around some

11. See Schmitter, Philippe, "Still the Century of Corporativism?" in *Review of Politics,* 25 (January 1973), and his important
book *Interest Conflict and Political Change in Brazil* (Stanford:
Stanford University Press, 1971); also Stepan, Alfred, *The State
and Society: Peru in Comparative Perspective,* forthcoming from
Princeton University Press. See especially chapters 1 and 2.

12. See Stepan, Alfred, *op. cit.,* where corporativism is *not*
inappropriately generalized to describe all authoritarian regimes.
See also, in Schmitter's book, cited above, the specifications made
in describing corporative relations between the state and civil society
and among parts of the latter.

specific policy or issue. In bureaucratic-authoritarian politics these semiformal structures substitute for an organization that is more stable and representative of class interests, namely parties. Particularly when regimes are centralized and positions at the top are decisive in the articulation of interests (Mexico, Chile, Brazil, Peru), bureaucratic rings seem to constitute the form of political linkage that establishes connections between civil society and the state. The linkage is not very stable, since the key official can be dismissed and the ring thereby broken.[13]

These formal aspects of the juncture between the state and civil society should not obscure the characteristics of the state in contemporary Latin America which we have already pointed out. The state is the expression of the dynamism of business enterprises and of the classes that control them as they operate in a context in which bureaucracies and the regulative and organizational capacities of the state are expanding. The basic ideology of the state is fundamentally "developmentalism." In view of the explicit ends of economic growth and national grandeur, the exploitation of workers, if not openly defended by the state, is justified by the argument that the tightening of belts is necessary "at the moment" so that "in the future" the results of this economy may be redistributed. We do not endorse studies of Latin American corporativism that see in it a "profound cultural trend," consonant with that society's patrimonialist structures. These structures were real in another and bygone situation, but in the current period of industrial-financial capitalist development, an insistence on the "necessity" of the corporative form in Latin American political relations seems to us an anachronistic and conservative point of view. When corporativist forms exist, and there are circumstances in which they do, they express the pact of dominion among

13. See especially, Cardoso, F. H., "A questão do Estado no Brasil," in *Autoritarismo e Democratização* (Rio de Janeiro, Paz e Terra, 1975).

classes trying to implant capitalist development, and the opposition which these attempts encounter in the political movements of subordinate classes.

Instead of insisting on the immutability of the "cultural dimension" and historical roots of corporativism, it seems to us that what is important is an understanding of the essence of contradiction between interests of people and current style of development, between the state and the nation. In these relationships of opposition, if any cultural dimension exists and carries significance, it is what Gramsci called a relationship of hegemony: the capacity to rule. The effective battle is not between corporativism and the democratic tradition. It is between technocratic elitism and a vision of the formative process of a mass industrial society which can offer what is popular as specifically national and which succeeds in transforming the demand for a more developed economy and for a democratic society into a state that expresses the vitality of truly popular forces, capable of seeking socialist forms for the social organization of the future.

Name Index

Subject Index